GUIDEBOOK

SEASONS OF HOPE

Creating

and Sustaining

Catholic

Bereavement

Groups

GUIDEBOOK

SEASONS OF HOPE

Creating

and Sustaining

Catholic

Bereavement

Groups

M. Donna MacLeod

ave maria press AmP notre dame, indiana

© 2007 by M. Donna MacLeod, RN, MSN

Founded in 1865, Ave Maria Press is a ministry of the Indiana Province of Holy Cross.

www.avemariapress.com

ISBN-10 1-59471-111-9   ISBN-13 978-1-59471-111-4

Cover and text design by John Carson.

Printed and bound in the United States of America.

To Erynne Lee MacLeod,
a cherished child
who loved Jesus
and now lives with him.

CONTENTS

"*Seasons of Hope* Prayer"

Our Father,
in this season of sorrow,
we turn to you.
Weakened with sadness,
we shed tears beyond number.
May those you send to help us
bring your love and consolation.

In this season of sorrow,
we lift up our broken hearts to you.
Heal us with your tender mercy and
make this a season of hope.
Trusting in your infinite kindness,
we ask this of you
with the Son and the Holy Spirit.

Amen

ACKNOWLEDGMENTS

My heartfelt thanks to all who helped shape the *Seasons of Hope Guidebook* and *Participant Journals*, particularly the clergy, friends, family, and bereaved who believe as I do that this work will enrich our parishes.

Sacred Heart Church of Hopedale, Massachusetts, hosted the first version of the bereavement group in the 1990s. Father Daniel R. Mulcahy, Jr. and Father Raymond M. Goodwin welcomed the ministry, Joe and Barbara Grillo helped out, and many enjoyed the sessions and asked for more.

Seasons of Hope in its present form was launched at Sacred Heart Church in Medford, Oregon, in 2004. Much refining was done thanks to my teammates and friends, Father Liam Cary and Mary Murphy, who facilitated the sessions with me, and Kathy Wallis and Barbara Halvorsen, who joined the team later. Special thanks also to Marie Carnegie, Cliff Downey, Joyce Farrell, Eleanor Geddes, Barbara Halvorsen, Doug Howat, Carol King, Joan Linkogle, Kathy Mannino, Marjorie Moore, Helen Puccetti, Annabelle Roberts, Sharon Roberts, and Arnold Widmer who gave valuable feedback on the program and *Participant Journals* pages they received each week. Some shared the journals with friends and family near and far, a testament to their appeal.

The enthusiasm and expertise of the Ave Maria Press professionals are greatly appreciated, especially those of Eileen Ponder, Bob Hamma, and Keri Suarez. Special thanks also to manuscript readers Linda Bowman, Dione and Larry Callahan, Meganne and Colt Duckworth, Nancy Mann, Helen Pride, and Barbara Wasnewsky for practical suggestions, and Mary Murphy and

Sister Mary Pat Naumes for an eye to spiritual matters and Church doctrine.

My husband Bryan's wisdom, love, and generous spirit greatly influenced this work. I treasure the input of our daughter Meganne, who remains a constant source of love and support, and the memory of our dear Erynne, whose death opened my heart to all who mourn.

A Pastor's Perspective

When I came to Sacred Heart Church as pastor, Donna MacLeod made known to me her work with the bereaved in New England. Later her desire—and mine—for a faith-based support group here came to fruition with *Seasons of Hope*. By then Donna had chaired our pastoral council and coordinated our Disciples in Mission program, so I had ample experience of her considerable talents as a planner, organizer, and motivator. As I expected, she put them to good use expanding the New England version of *Seasons of Hope* and implementing it in our parish.

What most drew me to Donna's vision for *Seasons of Hope* was its explicitly Catholic foundation. In contrast to secular support groups for the grieving, *Seasons of Hope* puts Jesus at the center and invites participants to entrust their loss and loneliness to him within the abundant consoling wisdom of our Catholic tradition. Every session builds on a well-chosen scripture foundation and invites participants to share their experiences in a context of devotion to Mary and the Saints.

Having just lost my mother, I was a natural candidate for *Seasons of Hope*. Its well-structured format enhanced our efforts as facilitators. When the sessions came to a close, I'd grown quite attached to my fellow group members and hated to see our time together end—as did all of us who took part. I hope the

Lord will extend the consolation he brought us to all others who take up this work of renewal and peace.

Father Liam Cary
Pastor
Sacred Heart Church
Medford, Oregon

INTRODUCTION

Welcome to *Seasons of Hope*

Dear Ministers to the Bereaved,

Who among us can lose a loved one and remain the same? No one I know. The pain of mourning is a powerful catalyst. If my daughter Erynne had survived cancer in 1988, the *Seasons of Hope* ministry would not exist today. For years, my nursing career brought me to the dying and their families. What they taught me about grief, however, was insufficient. I had to walk the road of mourning myself to truly understand.

Although each grief journey is unique, kindred feelings flow among those of us who know devastating loss firsthand. When we entrust our grief-stricken selves to the Lord Jesus Christ, the healer of our souls, untold grace unfolds. We become a blessing to others who mourn. Some, like you and me, make it possible for his Church to reach out to the bereaved with a support group that truly consoles. Through four unique six-week seasons (offerings) of *Seasons of Hope* each year, we link the bereaved with the Church, other parishioners of faith, and the Almighty in a most remarkable way.

Seasons of Hope groups are designed for easy adaptation in any parish whether it's in the heart of a city or on a winding country road. To help you get started, Part I of this *Guidebook* covers frequently asked questions:

- How do you assess the need for a bereavement group in the parish?
- What's the approval process?
- What does it take to organize *Seasons of Hope*?
- What can you do to invite the bereaved?
- What is faith sharing about?
- What do facilitators do?
- How does fellowship fit in?

Here you will find helpful pointers about weekly sessions to apply to the four seasons. This section also explores the basics about the *Participant Journals*, the *Guidebook*'s four companion booklets that enhance group sessions and personal growth through home activities.

In Part II of this book, each Footprint presents a single session of *Seasons of Hope* and serves as an easy-to-use script to lead a group. Each of the twenty-four sessions encourages participants with a lesson from Jesus about loss. Instead of focusing on a topic of grief, each *Seasons of Hope* session explores mourning through scripture, prayer, reflection, activities, and faith sharing. This is a tradition that shows God's love is given, fostering a deeper appreciation of the Catholic Church.

The appendix has tools that make your preparation easier: a sample brochure, at-a-glance outlines of sessions and journals, suggested sound recordings, and a resource list of helpful books and Web sites.

When parishioners ask why *Seasons of Hope* is offered, smile! *Seasons of Hope* parishes recognize Christ's call to console the mourning. Through it adults of all ages find Christ on their journey of sorrow. They have an opportunity to support each other and build up the faith community.

Whether your participants seek the deeper meaning of their grief or simply need consolation, you will find that *Seasons of Hope* comforts through the Church's teachings and provides fresh ways to cope with sorrow. And for those in your group who are weary of feeling alone, it comforts beyond measure.

Jesus Christ embodies compassion. As you strive to imitate him in your ministry, may you discover his face among those who mourn. With *Seasons of Hope* groups, you can say to them with confidence, "Come and be comforted!"

In Christ,
M. Donna MacLeod

PART
ONE

About
Seasons of Hope

ONE

The Decision

It's personal.

Deciding to offer a Christ-centered support group for your parish is a decision that will change lives! The noble act of reaching out to the bereaved comes to us from Jesus, our Savior. He tells us in the Sermon on the Mount: "Blessed are those who mourn, for they will be comforted" (Mt 5:4). He decided that it would come to pass. We are simply his instruments. But what a privilege!

The call to minister to the grieving has already awakened within you; otherwise, this *Seasons of Hope Guidebook: Creating and Sustaining Catholic Bereavement Groups* would not have found its way into your hands. Bereavement outreach in the parish may currently be your life's work. Perhaps now is the time to offer a group or bring a fresh approach to meetings. Or maybe you're one of the first in your parish to recognize the need for a support group that gathers the bereaved together in Christ's name to share their faith, to find healing, and to be enriched by the consoling traditions of our Church—all worthy pursuits that stimulate the imagination. Think of all those who will benefit. What parish is spared dealing with death and dying and funeral rites that may leave many feeling bereft? What about the deaths that parishioners encounter beyond the community of faith?

If you're like me, the death of a loved one broadsided you. Your pain is a powerful catalyst in Christ's hands; he heals your

crushed spirit so that it soars again. You see clearly in your midst those who need consoling. The silence of their suffering touches your heart. Our hearts are lifelines to the Lord. The Catechism of the Catholic Church tells us: "The heart is our hidden center, beyond the grasp of our reason and of others; only the Spirit of God can fathom the human heart and know it fully. The heart is the place of decision . . ." (CCC 2563). Trust it. Perhaps it is where we truly discern the voice of God.

Mother Teresa of Calcutta had a discerning heart. Her life's calling to serve the suffering poor might never have been realized if she had not stooped down to pick up that first dying person on the street. She could have walked on by, for surely she was already engaged in worthy service to God, but she chose to help that woman. She decided, and she acted on that decision. The face of Christ shone from those broken souls of Calcutta as surely as it radiates from our brothers and sisters who mourn. So if you wonder whether one person can make a difference, just remember Mother Teresa.

God also picks ordinary members of the clergy, religious, and lay people to accomplish his goals. With *Seasons of Hope* groups, good people like you can bring Christ into the lonely suffering of the bereaved in our Church. Let's see how it's done.

It's about the community of Christ.

The parish is as complicated as any corporate bureaucracy when it comes to making decisions. You may be in a position to witness parish politics either "make or break" efforts to initiate new programs, or you may be outside that arena. I learned firsthand that timing is of the essence. Doors will open if you're in stride with God's time. Pray that you are.

Pray that your pastor, parish administrator (PA), or parish life coordinator (PLC) is too, because he or she is likely the ultimate decision maker in the parish. Most pastors, PAs, and PLCs today have heavy assignments and little time to spare. That doesn't mean yours won't be open to innovation. These leaders often deal with grieving families and, as people of compassion, they see that losing a loved one breaks many hearts and wounds

many a spirit. Your parish leader has likely suffered through losing a dear one, which might color the response when you approach him or her about the need for a bereavement group.

Think positively. Whether you're a staff person or a volunteer with a calling, parish leaders usually respond positively to ideas that are well thought out, especially when an action-plan is included. They must also perceive a need for a ministry. If you discover that your pastor, PA, or PLC has already decided a faith sharing group for grieving parishioners is needed, thank God and skip to the next chapter!

Most of us have to do some legwork. Sometimes parish leaders want a fact-finding committee to weigh the pros and cons. Ask to be on it. Or you may be asked to investigate and report back. Whether you approach this alone or with a committee, be prepared to present a strong case.

The rest of this chapter will help you build that case. It uses questions that parish leaders and their advisers might pose while making a decision about *Seasons of Hope*. Your detective work connects you to staff and lay leaders you'll work with in the future. Enjoy the encounters and know that the Lord is with you every step of the way!

Factors That Influence the Decision

 ### *How many parishioners die annually?*

Research the last three years. A staff member is usually responsible for recording deaths for parish and diocesan records. The official book or computer file shows the name of the deceased, age, date of death, family contact/funeral director information, and other comments. The numbers give you a starting point. Then you can figure out if a widow, widower, or parents are left behind, but be aware that some potential participants (family members and friends) won't be obvious.

 *Is aging a factor in the parish?*

You probably have a good feel for the makeup of the parish simply by attending Masses scheduled at different times on the weekend. For hard statistics, check out a recent parish census that includes the homebound and residents of assisted living facilities who can't attend Mass.

Chances are that a parish top-heavy with elders has more funerals per year than a community dominated by young families. Be inclusive in your thinking. My last *Seasons of Hope* group sprang from a task force studying the needs of seniors, but participants ranged in age from thirty-something on up.

What about deaths beyond the parish?

My experience shows that many who seek group support have lost a loved one from outside the parish. How do you get a handle on how many there might be? A helpful parish secretary is a godsend. If weekend Mass petitions include the names of deceased who are distant relatives of parish members, the secretary probably gathered the information. The names may even be posted with those of deceased parishioners in the weekly bulletin that parishioners take home.

Ask about requests for Mass intentions. If the Book of Remembrance is used in November, find out if it is popular. Parishioners who seek these forms of honoring their loved ones may be drawn to a group.

What is currently available?

It's good to talk with the staff or volunteers who help families prepare for a funeral. A parish may offer a variety of ministries that don't include a support group experience for the bereaved. A Catholic women's group might help with an after-the-funeral gathering. A home visit ministry may send condolence cards and contact widows and widowers.

Don't worry if a faith sharing group for the grieving doesn't exist in your parish. Starting *Seasons of Hope* from scratch is the simplest path of all. A new program gets attention and draws volunteers interested in serving the bereaved. On the other hand, your parish may have a comprehensive bereavement ministry. Contact the coordinator to learn what services are in place. If a faith sharing group is in the planning stage, your involvement may guarantee that *Seasons of Hope* happens.

What about those of you who currently run a support group as a staff person or volunteer? Do you use a secular format that emphasizes stages of grief and coping skills? Or perhaps your group has an open forum and social focus. These efforts are important, but many times a similar program is available in the community. Why not give parishioners a spiritual lift and a route to the Lord through their darkest hours?

Consider the benefits of *Seasons of Hope.*

- It's centered on Jesus Christ and grounded in the teachings of the Catholic Church.
- It explores mourning by using scripture, prayer, reflection, activities, and faith sharing.
- It gives the bereaved an opportunity to come together to share in God's love.
- It fosters healing and spiritual growth.
- It's a nurturing link to fellow parishioners of faith.
- It offers a home journal to continue the weekly scripture story.
- It provides four seasons consisting of six sessions each (twenty-four different themes).

What about community resources?

Instead of offering a bereavement group, some parishes refer parishioners to local support groups. The grief work model used by community-based organizations has merit and is suited for

PART

ONE

nondenominational settings. I ran such a program for hospice, so I can attest to its value. Such offerings for the bereaved aren't meant to delve into matters of the soul. That responsibility truly lies with the parish.

Does a faith sharing group fit the plans of the parish?

Every parish has some form of strategic plan for the future. Depending on the leadership style of parish leaders, the plan may exist in their minds alone, in the job descriptions of the staff, or in a formal document devised in concert with an advisory council that represents parishioners. Any way you look at it, a new offering like *Seasons of Hope* must fit the perceived need of the parish and the timeline of current and upcoming projects.

In regard to future plans, the people in the know are the clergy, pastoral staff, and advisory councils (pastoral, administrative, and finance). If your parish communicates well with church members, plans may be posted on a bulletin board, or a Web site, or published in a newsletter or the weekly bulletin. It helps to review these sources before you contact the resource people.

To get an overview of scheduled parish events, investigate which meeting rooms are available in the months ahead. It may be premature to reserve space for *Seasons of Hope*, but take note of available slots that fit the six sessions per season. Each session, including fellowship, takes about two hours. Add a little time for setup and cleanup.

For my last group, Sunday afternoon was the only time the parish hall was available. That worked perfectly for retirees and those with full-time jobs. Participants didn't have to drive at night, and had ample parking and access to on-site childcare.

Who will do the work?

In Jesus' day, the harvest was plentiful but the laborers were few (Mt 9:37). Things haven't changed much, have they? Be

prepared for the show-stopping question: "Who is going to do this program?" Relax. It doesn't take an army. You want a facilitator to organize and preside at the weekly sessions. Your best bet is a proven leader who can facilitate faith sharing and attract others to the ministry. My guess is you, or someone you know, will fit the bill. So the rest is easy.

It takes only one facilitator (preferably with a "quiet" partner) for up to twelve participants. If a larger group is expected, have a back-up facilitator on hand. Some parishes like to preregister or limit the number of participants beforehand to match the group size to the facilitators and the available space.

If your parish takes part in a national program like RENEW or Disciples in Mission, trained facilitators for faith sharing groups are in your midst. Some of them have lost a loved one and might like to assist with a *Seasons of Hope* group. Don't forget to recruit a few who just want to pitch in and help. No doubt, their gifts and talents will come in handy. Having resource people at hand, in addition to your talents, helps the cause.

I find that the bereaved are best served when an ordained or a professionally trained lay ecclesial minister is part of the team. Because of the spiritual nature of the program and the deep wounds of the bereaved, having the wisdom of ministers of faith is a true blessing. This is not the typical faith sharing group that delves into issues of evangelization; rather, the sharing is deeply personal and soul-bearing. It is not a counseling session either, but time and again I've witnessed how a few words about God from a learned priest, deacon, or lay minister can ease the burden the bereaved carry.

On a personal note, I've had the privilege of offering *Seasons of Hope* with the support of enthusiastic priests. Each had his own style and approach to sessions. One preferred to welcome and offer prayer and words of wisdom "at will," and others shared directly in the facilitating. Each wondered if he could squeeze such a commitment into his life. I asked them to leave the planning to the team and just come. Concern would melt away at the first session when they saw the face of Christ among the participants. That awesome blessing kept them coming back. They soon realized the benefit and grace of consoling so

PART ONE

many parishioners simultaneously. The people also appreciated their presence. What a great use of the precious time God gives them!

It may take some convincing to get your pastor, PA, PLC, or other member of the parish pastoral staff to come onboard, but don't be afraid to ask. If his or her involvement becomes a deal breaker, *Seasons of Hope* can simply be offered with volunteer lay leaders alone.

What will Seasons of Hope *cost each season?*

A fiscally responsible parish looks at a program's price tag during the decision phase. So expect some questions. Here are basic items to consider:

- Books: *Seasons of Hope Guidebook*s (one per teammate); *Participant Journals* (one per participant and teammate each season.)
- Publicity materials: brochures, bulletin inserts, posters
- Session items: nametags, pencils, focal point, paper goods for refreshments

This bare-bones' list works well for our team and keeps costs to a minimum. It's simple to enhance the room with items from home or the parish (for example, a bell and a timer). We bring refreshments the first session and invite participants to pick a week to contribute a snack. If you aren't comfortable asking, include an estimate for snacks in the expense column.

On occasion, a pamphlet might be suggested for a session, but a cost-free alternative is given. Music is also optional. The music ministry or youth minister may have CDs or cassettes to borrow. If participants don't have bibles, the religious education director might have some to lend, or try the charismatic prayer group. Any attempt to keep expenses down will benefit everyone involved.

If defraying costs is necessary to launch the program, each participant could pay for his or her *Participant Journal* (or a

PART

ONE

portion of its cost). If the program is open to nonparishioners, charging them a fee is a possibility. The rationale here is that parishioners contribute to expenses by financial support to the church.

Consider how many times a year to offer *Seasons of Hope*. You could do as many as four seasons a year. Each season is a distinct stand-alone offering that fits the needs of new and returning members.

 ### *What benefits can you expect from* **Seasons of Hope?**

Churchgoers will be happy that your parish offers *Seasons of Hope*. It tells them that church leaders, like you, have a hand on the pulse of parish life. Christ wants those who mourn to be comforted, and you give example by bringing him into their suffering. Expect the parish to be blessed because participants bond as Catholic people, building a strong sense of community that fosters stewardship.

Also consider how *Seasons of Hope* might benefit those who attend. If a neighboring parish offers the program, by all means, talk to the people involved. You will hear how fellowship with kindred souls helps lessen loneliness—a major concern after the loss of a loved one. Comfort also comes from the spiritual benefits of focusing on Christ.

Group members from Sacred Heart in Medford, Oregon, had these things to say following the winter 2005 sessions:

- "I learned some ways to bring more prayer into my grieving and remembering my loved ones. I also found some positive ways to help others and myself."
- "My time with Seasons of Hope has been so, so sweet and great! And the Participant Journal helps me reach into my soul and write concerns that I had during my husband's dying."
- "Seasons of Hope lets me reflect on my grieving and be with the Lord."

- "It helps me to know that others want to talk about and remember their loved ones. I learned that the Lord does not leave us to grieve alone."

Don't be surprised if bereavement team members discover blessings in their own lives. We did. My pastor, Father Liam Cary, writes most eloquently about the benefits:

> The best evidence I have for the value of *Seasons of Hope* is that none of us wanted it to end. Our Sunday afternoons together brought a compassionate appreciation for one another's struggles to let go of a loved one. We learned to let others into our struggle and to enter gently into theirs, to take strength and to give it. The program proved to be true to its name: we had helped each other to hope.

Presenting the Findings

Before you (and perhaps a fact-finding committee) present your assessment to the pastoral staff (and possibly the advisory councils), it's best to organize your thoughts. I like to outline the major points and develop a handout for the meeting. You might use the nine questions listed under "Factors That Influence the Decision" as the headers for your findings. As with most committees, expect to submit a formal report that includes a recommendation.

It's easy to recommend *Seasons of Hope*. It works! Expect a question or two about the format. This *Guidebook* gives enough detail to boost your confidence. Plus you have a Footprint of each session and the seasons' outlines (Sessions-at-a-Glance and Journals-at-a-Glance) in the appendix to explain meetings and the home journal feature.

Christ is counting on you, so speak from your heart and present the facts. He will inspire your words. Then relax. When the decision comes to move forward, the next chapter (First Steps) shows you where to begin.

TWO

First Steps

How often do good ideas for your parish go undeveloped because no one knows quite where to start? You need clear vision to begin a faith sharing group for the bereaved and the proper tools for the job. The *Seasons of Hope Guidebook* and *Participant Journal* booklets provide the vision and proven means to accomplish a Christ-centered program that comforts those who mourn.

The rich diversity within the Church across America is awesome to behold. Each parish envisions *Seasons of Hope* through the lens of its unique history and culture, yet the steps to creating the program rely on common God-given gifts and talents of parish leaders. Whether you're a seasoned facilitator of a bereavement ministry, a novice, or a supporter of the efforts, the following tips answer common questions on how to accomplish the mission.

Tasks of the Facilitator (about eight weeks before sessions begin)

Where do you start?

When you undertake a ministry, look to the life of Jesus Christ for inspiration. Time and again scripture shows that the

PART ONE

Lord reverently prayed to the Father as he began and carried out his mission of salvation. The *Seasons of Hope* ministry is deeply rooted in prayer that seeks God's will. God wants to comfort those who mourn, and the program is an effective way to bring Christ to those who seek him in their grief.

As you prepare for this special outreach to mourners, seek ways that the parish can pray for the ministry. A powerful opportunity during Mass is the Prayer of the Faithful. A petition could be added such as "For those who mourn in our parish—let our new bereavement ministry bring consolation." Check with the parish staff about how to go about this. If you attend daily Mass and can offer a petition from the pew, do so. Writing your request in the book of petitions also reaps the benefit of communal prayer.

Meanwhile, continue to seek God's grace in your own prayer and know that others across the country are praying for you and your parish ministry. We ask God to pour out the Holy Spirit upon you so that you may be fully equipped to build his kingdom through acts of compassion for those who mourn.

What is the pastor's, parish administrator's, or parish life coordinator's perspective?

The Christ-centered nature of the program, with its use of scripture and Catholic traditions, make it the perfect forum for a pastor, PA, or PLC to share personal knowledge and love of God with the brokenhearted. In them, he or she encounters the suffering face of Christ. When your parish's leader believes that caring for those who mourn is as much a part of the Church's mission as the sacraments and spreading the gospels, he or she will approve the formation of the *Seasons of Hope* ministry. How active your pastor, PA, or PLC becomes depends on how creative that person is with scheduling and his or her desire and ability to personally reach those who mourn. To launch the program, the pastor, PA, or PLC appoints a capable facilitator who understands the concerns of the bereaved. The ideal

candidate is energetic, faith filled, organized, and creative, as well as a proven leader and a person of great compassion.

The facilitator could be a staff member who oversees family life, senior ministry, parish nursing, or spiritual aspects of the community, or an interested volunteer who has leadership skill or professional qualifications. A volunteer leader would report to a pastoral adviser—either the pastor or a designated member of the pastoral staff. In this way, the *Seasons of Hope* ministry always receives pastoral guidance.

A pastor and/or pastoral staff member stirs up community interest in the pre-program phase each season. Whether attendance is encouraged through a homily, Mass announcements, a personal column in the bulletin, invitation letters, or by recommending *Seasons of Hope* to individuals in need, the wholehearted support of the pastoral staff sends a positive message to parishioners.

The pastor, PA, or PLC can also make a difference at sessions by welcoming participants at the beginning of each season, or stopping by during fellowship. A group is specially blessed if such pastoral leaders lead prayer, co-facilitate, or join the faith sharing circle to share wisdom and compassion. This public and prayerful support from leadership strengthens the ministry.

What does it take to get Seasons of Hope rolling?

Ministering to the bereaved requires gifts, talents, and trust in the benevolence of God. If you are the facilitator, take a moment to give thanks. The Lord has called you and that will bring you joy and peace.

As facilitator you:

- organize the ministry,
- seek teammates,
- implement each season,
- and involve your pastoral adviser and teammate(s) in decisions and tasks.

PART
ONE

The table below is a guide to launching the first season. The timeline is just a guide. Feel free to add to it, omit some tasks, change the order, or revisit it to plan for next season.

Preparation Timeline

Facilitator Tasks

When	What
Eight to ten weeks before the first season begins	Meet with pastoral adviser
	Determine target population
	Decide *Seasons of Hope* year
	Book facility for year
	Order team *Guidebooks* and journals
	Arrange Prayer of the Faithful intentions
	Explore speaker campaign at weekend Masses
	Contact organizations to arrange *Seasons of Hope* speaker
	Recruit ministry teammate(s)

Team Tasks

When	What
About six weeks before the first season begins	Plan promotion and needed teamwork
	Provide information to staff and clergy
	Create/display brochures

	Make signs; post promotional ones
	Submit all bulletin announcements
	Compile mailing list/mail invitations
	Investigate childcare options
	Begin Prayer of the Faithful at Masses
Four weeks before	Plan details of weekly sessions*
	Discuss role of facilitator(s) (see chapter 3)
	Decide tasks at sessions*
	Order *Participant Journals*
	Continue Prayer of the Faithful
One to three weeks before	Speak at organizations and weekend Masses
	Register participants by phone, e-mail, or mail
	Arrange for room setup and refreshments*
	Get bibles for group use*
	Continue Prayer of the Faithful

*More details in chapter 4, page 65

The rest of this chapter addresses questions that arise during preseason planning, team building, and promotion.

Mapping Out the Ministry

 When should you meet with the pastoral adviser?

The earlier you share your vision for the year with your pastoral adviser, the better. Most of this section requires approval from parish leadership, so seek advice up front.

What about Prayers of the Faithful?

Any *Seasons of Hope* activity that takes place at Mass needs pastoral approval.

What will the Seasons of Hope *ministry offer this year?*

You know that bereaved parishioners are in your midst, so what can you offer them? An active *Seasons of Hope* ministry has four unique seasons to draw participants each year.

Is the order of seasons important?

No. Seasons are numbered one through four for ease of reference—not because one builds upon another. Each season welcomes newcomers and former participants with unique material.

Who should get a Guidebook *and* Journal?

Seasons of Hope Guidebooks are an essential tool for the ministry's decision makers, promoters, and teammates. Provide the companion *Participant Journal* booklets to round out everyone's understanding of the ministry. Group participants need the journal of the season for sessions and home activities. Clarify with the pastoral adviser whether the booklets are a gift to parishioners (and possibly nonparishioners) or whether a donation to defray costs is expected. If donations are collected, discuss cost per booklet and ask how to handle the proceeds.

How do you predict how many will come?

Predicting is tricky business. Funerals per year may identify grieving families, but not everyone will want to join a

bereavement group. You also need to think about those who lose someone beyond the parish. How can you reach them? You could estimate five to ten participants, the average size of a support group. Some parishes choose the group size and register accordingly. Turnout, however, can exceed your wildest expectation even with preregistration, so order booklets carefully.

 ## Who gets invited to the group?

Seasons of Hope is for those who long to find Christ in mourning, yet more is involved. Your pastoral adviser will know if your diocese encourages shared resources. If so, your group sessions will probably welcome participants from other parishes (another factor for your booklet order). On the other hand, some churches offer *Seasons of Hope* to connect their own parishioners. I have led open and parish-only offerings, and each proved popular. Open sessions also drew non-Catholics.

When a group is limited in size because of available facilitators or seating, who attends can become an issue. Do you reserve openings solely for parishioners? Decide beforehand with your pastoral adviser.

 ## What is the best way to offer sessions?

The *Seasons of Hope* design has the group meet for six consecutive weeks (one season). It takes commitment to come each week, but commitment creates trust among participants and a positive atmosphere for faith sharing.

Where do you hold sessions?

If at all possible, keep the same schedule and setting for the season. Parish facilities work nicely for *Seasons of Hope* groups of all sizes. The site gives a clear message that the Church cares about its bereaved. A parish hall is convenient and usually can

be easily accessed by everyone, including those with special needs. Chairs and parking are plentiful, and often childcare and kitchen facilities are available. If you book a room at the parish, add time before and after the two-hour session for setup and cleanup.

If a parish facility is unavailable, a home setting is an alternative worth pursuing. The home should be a reasonable distance from the church. Faith Sharing groups that have as many as eight people do well in the average-size house. Since homeowners get ill and have emergencies, also have an alternate site and a plan to notify participants.

What makes a good meeting room?

Whether in a parish facility or a home, select a room that fits the size of your anticipated group and has space to mingle during fellowship. You want a room that has privacy, adequate lighting, climate control, and electric outlets to handle music players and coffee pots. Also consider whether noise from outside the room will pose a problem.

What time is best?

Each parish selects a time for its first program based on the availability of the team and site. Ask your adviser about parish events that may affect promotion or attendance. The time you select will influence who comes. The employed may prefer groups in late afternoon, the evening, or on weekends. Those who don't drive after dark prefer daytime sessions.

What about ministry expenses?

Seasons of Hope is a low-budget ministry, but expenses do come up. The adviser may have you contact the business manager to submit receipts for reimbursement. Also discuss

whether brochures and signs should be copied on office machinery or sent out for printing.

 What other advice might a facilitator need?

If you plan to recruit volunteers to help with the ministry, talk with the pastoral adviser about your choices or ask for names of possible candidates. Once you meet with the adviser, you can set the ministry wheels in motion.

Building a Team

 How do you recruit bereavement ministers?

It is fair to say that Jesus could have conducted his ministry on his own, but he chose to surround himself with helpers. You don't have to undertake a ministry alone either. Although *Seasons of Hope* doesn't require a crowd of bereavement ministers to accomplish its goal, having a companion or two on the journey blesses your efforts.

Opportunities to serve go beyond running sessions and facilitating faith sharing. Some prefer to help with preseason planning, publicity, and mailings. During the season, some are greeters, registrars, or readers of the Word, while others are involved with refreshments, setup, or cleanup. The trick to building a compatible team is to welcome all who want to serve, find something that interests them, and then let them do it.

Recruitment can begin with a bulletin announcement. When you invite the community to help with *Seasons of Hope*, you spread the word about it. It's a perfect way to reach newcomers and parishioners who want to serve the bereaved.

(**SAMPLE** Recruitment Announcement)

Seasons of Hope **is coming in June!**
Volunteers needed.

A unique Christ-centered support group for the
bereaved will be offered at Sacred Heart on
six Mondays this summer. The facilitators would
love some helpers to join in. It's not a big-time
commitment, but your effort will help many. Please
contact (name and phone number)
for ways to get involved.

Another good starting point is people you know. Prayerfully reflect on those who have adjusted well to losing a loved one. Rejoice if one comes to mind who has strong faith in God, has compassion and patience with others, listens well, keeps confidences, works well with you and others, and is available to serve. Such a person is a gift from God, so make that call!

You can seek input from parish staff, leaders of related ministries, or council members who represent the parish at large. The parish computer database may also have names of parishioners who indicate experience with bereavement ministry. Don't forget to invite a parish priest, deacon, or lay pastoral staff member with a recent loss or chaplaincy experience.

Once *Seasons of Hope* is underway, a new source of volunteers will exist in former participants. They know the benefits and may feel called to minister to others.

What's the best way to contact unknown candidates for the team?

Consider whether the culture of your parish tends to be formal. If so, send a letter of introduction before making "blind" calls to candidates you don't know. Here's an example:

(SAMPLE Invitation to Potential Team Member)

SACRED HEART CATHOLIC CHURCH

1234 Main Street • Anytown, USA
Phone: 123-4567 • Rectory: 123-4567

Dear _____,

Sacred Heart needs people of compassion to offer a *Seasons of Hope* faith sharing group to those who mourn. Leaders in the parish tell me that you have gifts and talents that could help the ministry make a difference. This summer, six sessions are planned for Mondays from June 11 through July 16.

Perhaps you would like to get involved. I will call in a week to discuss the details with you. Meanwhile, please keep *Seasons of Hope* in your prayers as you consider serving those in need of consolation.

Sincerely,
Mary Davis
Facilitator, *Seasons of Hope*

 Are phone calls a good approach?

Calling potential volunteers without a prior letter works nicely in some parishes. Let the person know that you represent the parish and how you came by his or her name, and say you are recruiting for the ministry.

Some want to hear about *Seasons of Hope* right then or may ask to meet with you. Some want information mailed to them. Others like time to think about the request. Either response gives the person an opportunity to discover how prepared and flexible you are. You also get a sense of the individual and his or her interest.

Expect to get at least one "No, thank you" during the search. Direct, decisive people know their limits and don't waste time. What a blessing for you! You don't need someone who will back out at the last minute. But before you let the person off the hook, find out if he or she knows of a potential volunteer. The response might be the lead you're looking for.

 ## What's the next step?

When someone expresses interest in the ministry, set up a meeting. I like to send a follow-up note.

(SAMPLE "Welcome to the Team" Letter)

SACRED HEART CATHOLIC CHURCH

1234 Main Street · Anytown, USA
Phone: 123-4567 · Rectory: 123-4567

Dear _____,

I am delighted you will join in our efforts at Sacred Heart to comfort those who mourn. As we discussed, the *Seasons of Hope* planning meeting is on Sunday, April 22 at 3:00 in the parish center. If you have any questions, feel free to call me at 555-xxxx.

Meanwhile, please keep *Seasons of Hope* and those we serve in your prayers.

In Christ,
Mary Davis
Facilitator, *Seasons of Hope*

 What happens at the prospective volunteer meeting?

Whether it's done one-on-one over a cup of coffee or with a group, share the Christ-centered approach of *Seasons of Hope* and what participants will gain. Use this chapter and the checklist in chapter 4 (page 65) to explain what the team does. Before you finish, confirm each person's desire to serve.

 What makes a good bereavement team?

Find a way to involve each volunteer, and your team will thrive. Working together for the Lord will bring joy to the ministry.

Team Tasks (about six weeks before season begins)

Promotion
 How do you get the word out?

Promotion is an important step to bring Christ to those who mourn. Know the gifts and talents of your team and involve them in getting the word out.

 What about a brochure?

A *Seasons of Hope* brochure (from a double-sided 8.5"x11" sheet) can be specific to a season or created for year-round use. Each column or panel has a job. Side one has a title, reasons why people like the ministry, and a blank middle panel (the back) for parish-specific information. Side two has the program overview, the design of sessions, and statements about the team. See the appendix for a sample (page 179) and visit www.avemariapress.com for a template to create your customized brochure.

Whether you use the sample text in the appendix or create your own, try different fonts, paperweights, and colors to find what best suits your offering. Add clip art or your church logo to the front panel if you like. Parchment stationery folds the best for brochures; however, it costs a little more than twenty-four-weight paper.

Strategically place your brochures. Use a clear, upright stand to get the brochures noticed on an information table. Think beyond the racks in the church, parish hall, and office. Brochures work best when they are coupled with a letter, a speaker campaign, or one-on-one contact.

Who else gets a brochure?

Start with the parish secretary, staff, and clergy, both active and retired. Also be sure to include the parish pastoral council and perhaps the finance council. If possible, present the brochure at pastoral staff and council meetings to answer questions and seek referrals.

If home visitors or a parish funeral planner work with the bereaved, seek their support and give them a supply of brochures. Funeral directors also can provide *Seasons of Hope* brochures to bereaved family members.

What about bulletin announcements?

Parish bulletin announcements can be an effective tool for reaching grieving members of the community, either directly or through friends. Find out the deadline for submissions, whether e-mail submissions are accepted and any other guidelines the parish has.

(Sample Bulletin Announcement)

> ### *Seasons of Hope*
> ### Bereavement Group to Begin
>
> If you're in need of consolation after losing a loved one, this Christ-centered faith sharing group is for you. It meets for six Mondays beginning June 11. Prayer, scripture, faith sharing, and fellowship begin at 10 a.m. For more details, pick up a *Seasons of Hope* brochure or call (add name and phone number).

 ## *What about posters?*

Check with the office staff about posting on bulletin boards. Some parishes assign space to each ministry. A good location to promote *Seasons of Hope* is any place where parishioners can pause to read the poster. The best design is simple yet catchy. Choose a prominent phrase and a concise message. Here's my favorite approach.

(Sample Wording of Poster)

> Come and Be Comforted
>
> # SEASONS OF HOPE
> A group for the bereaved
> begins
> June 11, 10 a.m.
> at
> The Parish Center, Meeting Room A
> *Please take a brochure!*

You don't have to be an artist or a computer whiz to make a poster, but why not ask someone with talent to donate what you need? A parish school often has a computer lab and an art teacher with students who do things for the church. Decide the number of posters needed, color preferences, lettering style, and design. An 8.5 x 11 size works well because it fits on most bulletin boards. Poster board or laminated paper holds up the best.

Besides promotional signs at church entrances, include the parish office and hall (even restrooms), the chapel entry, and ask about the school reception area, if available. Have extra signs to replace those that go home with parishioners. If the group meets at a parish facility, also make some "Welcome to *Seasons of Hope*" signs for the day of the program.

How about an invitation letter?

A pastoral letter to recently bereaved families is a powerful way to draw participants. You can verify when letters are delivered by mailing one to your own address. Feel free to adapt the following example to meet the needs of your parish.

(Sample Letter to the Bereaved)

 SACRED HEART CATHOLIC CHURCH

1234 Main Street • Anytown, USA
Phone: 123-4567 • Rectory: 123-4567

Dear _____,

We (I) extend to you our deepest sympathies for the loss of your
_____.

As you know, mourning the loss of someone you love is never easy, but there is hope. Our Sacred Heart parish community will host *Seasons of Hope,* a unique support group for the bereaved. This program, rooted in Catholic tradition, conveys God's consolation through scripture, prayer, reflection, and sharing our faith. I hope you and your family will read the enclosed brochure for details and prayerfully consider (my or our) invitation to come.

The group meets at the parish center for two hours each Monday morning for six weeks beginning June 11. Your reply—via the enclosed postcard or by calling 555-XXXX—by May 28 is appreciated.

Be uplifted knowing that the Lord blesses those who mourn. Surely, *Seasons of Hope* is a way to find him in our midst.

Peace in the Lord,

Fr. Larry Deagon
Pastor, Sacred Heart Catholic Church

Mary Davis
Facilitator, *Seasons of Hope*

Some participants who received a similar letter told me that the personal nature of the invitation encouraged them to come. A form letter would have been a turnoff. If registration by a self-addressed, stamped postcard is desired, mail the letter about six weeks before the season. State a deadline for reply.

(Sample Response Postcard)

SACRED HEART CATHOLIC CHURCH
1234 Main Street • Anytown, USA
Phone: 123-4567 • Rectory: 123-4567

We hope you and your family will join us at *Seasons of Hope*. To help us plan, please complete this card and return it by May 28. Thank you!

Name(s):_____

Contact's phone number: _____

Name of deceased and anniversary date:

_____

____ Childcare needed (Please list names and ages.)

_____   _____

_____   _____

____ Sorry, but I'm unable to attend.

Phone registration is another option. Make a short form or have index cards to take the information noted above.

Does a low response mean cancel the program?

No. Even a small group does God's work. Trust God, not the numbers. A meager response beforehand doesn't mean that those who receive the letter won't come! Plus your parish-wide promotion invites everyone. Many aren't on the mailing list because their loss occurred more than a year before or the deceased lived outside the parish, yet they may compose a good portion of the group whether they preregister or not.

Where can a mailing list come from?

The team usually compiles a mailing list. When parish death records have family information, the job is easy. Decide which months the list will cover (usually twelve) and copy the information. When death records omit contact information for relatives, the team plays detective. You can contact the parish's funeral planner; match names to a church directory, database, or telephone book; or call funeral directors.

Check your list with a long time parishioner or a ministry leader who makes home visits. Such a person often knows the deceased and family. Get the pastor's, parish administrator's, or parish life coordinator's input on the list, too. They know their flocks.

Should you investigate childcare options beforehand?

Yes. Childcare providers need to make plans, and you need to book the playroom. Seek a six-week commitment, but make the provider aware that the service depends on enrollment and walk-ins. Ask if the provider wants parents to call when a child will be absent.

🍃 *How about a speaking campaign?*

Presenting *Seasons of Hope* to the community bolsters participation. Early on, contact organizations and ministries that serve the bereaved and ask to be on the next agenda. A five-minute presentation works. Provide brochures and use one to highlight key points. Then take questions from the audience. Some who are present may need the support group, so invite them to come. Ask everyone to be ambassadors for *Seasons of Hope* and to pray for those who mourn.

🍃 *Which church groups do you approach?*

The pastoral council, Council of Catholic Women, Catholic Daughters, Knights of Columbus, Legion of Mary, senior's groups, prayer groups, adult formation groups, Bible studies, parent meetings for children in religious education and sacramental preparation programs, and RCIA teams and groups are all potential audiences for fruitful speaking engagements. Many other opportunities may exist in your parish. If a speaking opportunity can't be arranged, provide *Seasons of Hope* brochures for the various group leaders to distribute. Most will be happy to oblige.

🍃 *What about presentations at weekend Masses?*

Some churches encourage ministry speakers. A speakers' campaign a weekend or two before the season is ideal. Decide whether to host a registration table after Masses. A three-minute talk is the norm and one written from the heart is more powerful than rattling off dates and times. The speaker should practice with the church microphone beforehand, be certain to arrive in plenty of time that day and check in with the sacristan and/or priest celebrant to remind her or him that a ministry talk is planned for that Mass.

What about a church Web site?

Many parishes have a Web site that offers bulletin information or a parish calendar of events. It's a good way to advertise *Seasons of Hope*. If space allows, simply reformat the information in the brochure for use there. If you want a shorter announcement, reuse the bulletin notice.

How do you reach the bereaved who don't attend Mass regularly?

Some find it difficult to return to church after the funeral Mass of a loved one. Maybe the surroundings bring back sad memories or the person is angry with God about his or her loss. Whatever the reason, will parish and public announcements draw such people in? Maybe not, but the concern of a relative or friend could. During promotion, encourage parishioners to bring them to *Seasons of Hope*. Some parishes reach nonpracticing members through the local newspaper's community events page.

How do you handle inquiry calls?

Bereaved callers often have details of *Seasons of Hope* in hand. Most, in my experience, call to determine if the group is right for them. How you or your teammates respond may influence whether the caller joins the group.

What can you do? Be you. Find out why the person called. Listen with genuine interest as the story unfolds. Offer a kind word or two. Compassion shows the essence of a group experience better than any sales pitch.

 What's next?

You now have some tools and the basics on how to structure *Seasons of Hope*, recruit helpers, and rally support in the faith community. The next chapter focuses on the faith sharing experience.

THREE

Faith Sharing, Facilitators, and Fellowship

For some of us, losing a loved one is a powerful experience that can change the way we look at life. The intensity of our grief reaction and how long mourning will linger often depend on how close we were to the deceased, the history of that bond, and other losses we have suffered in the past.

Grief brings pain whether it is expressed through emotions, physical symptoms, or disturbing behaviors that prompt us to seek help. When we are people of faith, we may sense that our spirit is wounded as well. Although the consolation of Christ surrounds us during bereavement, the throes of grief can blind us to it.

This chapter lays the cornerstone for a Christ-centered *Seasons of Hope* group in your parish. It offers new and veteran bereavement ministers plenty of ideas about the essence of faith sharing, effective facilitating, and the healing power of fellowship.

PART ONE

The Essence of Faith Sharing

 Did Jesus leave us any clues on faith sharing?

Faith sharing is not something new. The final chapter of the Gospel of Luke gives us a glimpse of how Jesus shared the faith with his bereaved disciples. He appeared to two of them on the road to Emmaus while they were discussing his death and debating what had happened.

Even though the pair did not recognize their savior, Jesus asked a question that enabled them to pour out their grief. It seems he listened attentively to his disciples' sorrow and hope. Then he brought the scriptures to life, using it to strengthen their faith in him. The framework for bereavement faith sharing was born.

What is faith sharing?

Faith sharing is a process that lets us view mourning through the eyes of scripture. It helps us explore our losses and belief in God by relating to the story of Jesus and others in the Bible. In so doing, we open ourselves to Christ's consolation and healing.

What is the group etiquette for faith sharing?

A facilitator guides the process by keeping the focus on the questions and the Lord. A facilitator doesn't teach, preach, or advise. He or she creates a safe place for participants to express their feelings about loss and receive consolation. Participants are asked to commit to a simple code that demonstrates respect for the group and its individual members.

Group members agree to:

- show up and make it known if they can't attend,
- arrive on time,

PART

ONE

- treat others with respect,
- share their faith story and then let others talk,
- listen carefully,
- keep what is shared in confidence and within the group,
- and be open to God's message.

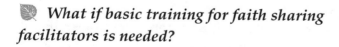 How many facilitators do you need for a group?

Faith Sharing works best if one facilitator poses questions to the group and guides the conversation when needed. A co-facilitator, who may be a facilitator trainee, serves as a "quiet" partner.

The quiet partner sits on the opposite side of the circle and surveys group dynamics. He or she signals the facilitator if anyone gets overlooked during the sharing, so all are included. The partner adds to faith sharing if desired, monitors the time, and serves as a back-up facilitator if an additional group is needed.

After the session, the facilitator and partner take time to review and evaluate in a supportive way their efforts during the group. They discuss what transpired and assess the process. They might want to switch roles for a session or two during a season. Most groups adjust easily, and quietly observing the group process can sharpen one's skill as a facilitator.

What if basic training for faith sharing facilitators is needed?

A variety of resources or training programs are available through parishes, diocesan offices, The National Catholic Ministry to the Bereaved, or a certified bereavement ministry consultant such as the author.

🍃 *Who seeks a bereavement faith sharing group?*

The simple answer is the bereaved among us who practice the faith and look to the Church for support during mourning. Some may read numerous self-help books about loss. Some seek counseling. Others attend a support group that emphasizes stages of grief and coping skills. Such groups are a great help with day-to-day matters, but many do not delve deeply into spiritual concerns or the journey of faith. For those who hunger for God's consolation from within the tradition of the Catholic Church, *Seasons of Hope* can nourish the soul.

Those of us who look to God for guidance tend to recognize signs of the divine in the world and in everyday life. Church may be the only place where we meet others who willingly acknowledge God's presence. Even in a parish setting, finding those who are comfortable sharing their faith can be a challenge.

When we come to a *Seasons of Hope* session, we are much like the disciples on the road to Emmaus. We too are people of faith who feel a need to talk about a deceased loved one. We may feel confused by our loss. Sorrow and hope drift through our thoughts. Like the Emmaus disciples, we may not recognize Christ in our midst or relate our trials of mourning to his suffering. Yet we want help. *Seasons of Hope* uses scripture to point us to the Lord, our consoler.

🍃 *Does a facilitator need a counseling degree?*

No. *Seasons of Hope* is a peer ministry that encourages those who have gone through mourning to minister to the newly bereaved. Experience with small groups or a faith sharing group is desirable though. If you're a person of hospitality and compassion, you ought to facilitate well. Your skill at speaking and listening as well as your experience with bereavement come into play as you encourage the group to journey together.

Some facilitators like to study works on group leading, grief theory, and mourning. (See resources in the appendix.) Some simply observe skilled facilitators who make the process look

easy. Do either of those tasks and more if you like. But the most important book for you to refer to is the book of your life—your own experience with loss, grief, and communicating with God and others.

Is there a spiritual dimension to facilitating?

Yes. Pray that God gives you what you need to do his will and that you are open to the brokenhearted people he sends you. Then trust. When I guide a group, I usually don't recall catchy phrases the experts find helpful in a pinch. I respond from the core of my being, from the sympathetic heart that God has given me. When you respect yourself and the participants in the circle, you allow the Holy Spirit to bring out the best in each of you.

What does a facilitator do?

As a facilitator, you invite participants to share their stories of loss with the group and, like Jesus on the road to Emmaus, you listen attentively.

What does attentive listening involve?

It means paying attention to the facts of the participant's story and the emotions expressed. Even when someone doesn't name feelings, body language often gives a hint. When needed, verify your perception by briefly reflecting back to that individual what you see and hear.

Your body language is also important. Facing the person and maintaining eye contact communicate interest and encourage sharing. Uncrossed arms and legs convey an attitude of openness to the speaker. Responding in a supportive manner to each participant fosters an atmosphere of acceptance. In such a climate, the group learns to trust the process.

 What are some tips for effective facilitating?

You want to guide the process without dominating it. Some facilitators like to initiate sharing by giving an example from their own loss. Sometimes that is necessary, but your comments will influence what participants say. Instead, use the *Seasons of Hope* question from the Footprint and let participants go where they need to go with it.

Your goal isn't to teach, give sermons, or talk a lot about yourself. You simply make sharing easy and enjoyable for others. With your support, the bereaved can minister to each other.

What's the best way to handle silence?

Don't fret when silence reigns. Many participants need time to think before they speak, so resist the urge to fill in the quiet. If the pause makes the group uncomfortable, repeat or rephrase the question or move on to another. If silence seems to have nothing to do with the question, get feedback on what is happening in the group.

Sometimes participants aren't comfortable sharing with the group, yet they return each week. Maybe their loss was recent and they are afraid that speaking will intensify their grief. With time, they usually open up. Others may be shy or simply reserved. They might benefit from some gentle coaxing. If such a person is nodding yes as another speaks, I might say to her, "You look like you can relate to that . . ."

Sometimes silent participants want to remain anonymous. Perhaps their loss involves suicide, murder, abortion, or a dreaded disease. Or they harbor deep-rooted ill feelings toward the deceased that they dare not share. If that kind of situation is revealed during faith sharing, it demands great sensitivity. The facilitator and any team members present must respond delicately, lending visible support without prying or asking for more from the participant than he or she seems prepared to share. You may want to talk with the participant outside the

group, possibly referring him or her to a specialty support group or a professional counselor. This is a good time to remember that as a facilitator you have access to a pastoral adviser who may have excellent insight on how to approach the situation.

How does a facilitator maximize sharing?

Each faith sharing group has a personality all its own. Like in any healthy relationship, participants become more comfortable with each other as time passes. You deal with several factors when you pose a question to the group. Initially, you respond to the individual who replies first, and then you ease others into sharing. After a few sessions, a healthy group needs less prompting from you to share with each other.

As you and the group listen to a faith story, whether it is heart wrenching or uplifting, the one speaking receives attention and a message of affirmation and acceptance from the group. Participants are receptive to questions when they sense that what they say will be valued. You can thank them for sharing with words, smiles, nods, or other gestures; just acknowledge and appreciate each participant. This encourages participants to affirm each other.

How do you handle emotional reactions in the group?

Some bereaved never join a group because speaking about their loss brings an emotional meltdown. Those who find the courage to attend have similar concerns. No matter how nicely you explain that the group is a safe place to let tears and emotions flow, participants struggle to control their grief reactions. When participants cry and their words get choked off, don't panic. And don't automatically pass a box of tissues to them unless they look for one. An unsought tissue is often interpreted as a signal to stop crying. Crying actually releases emotions, helping the person.

When someone can't go on talking, you can respect his or her grieving with quiet attention. If it feels right, offer a petition that lifts the person up to the Lord. Use whatever comes to you at the moment. I might say,

> Lord, our friend Lorraine is filled with sorrow right now.
> We lift her broken heart up to you. Bring peace to her.
> We ask in your name. Amen.

When your "Lorraine" has taken a deep breath and looks at you, you might concisely repeat her story before the meltdown to validate it with her and encourage her to go on. Whether her decision is to continue with the tale or decline, she discovers acceptance. The sad moment often is a great gift, because other participants generally speak up and relate to the person's grief.

 How do you set the pace for sharing?

It comes as a surprise to some participants when the mood of sharing is upbeat. Sharing the joy our deceased loved ones once brought is just as welcome during faith sharing as tears. No matter what the mood of the session, aim to finish the faith sharing segment on time. Have your partner signal when ten and five minutes remain. If everyone in the group hasn't spoken by then, you still have time to draw the quiet ones in.

 How do you keep the focus on Christ?

When a participant or the group wanders away from the posed question, a simple "We're getting off track. The question is . . . " usually does the trick.

How do you handle someone who starts to ramble?

Sometimes a participant rambles on and on, pouring out a story that clearly seems endless. People start to fidget. What do you do? Wait for the speaker to take a breath and then interrupt? Perhaps, but try to do it in a respectful way. Think about what Jesus would do.

Would he listen carefully? Would he reflect back the pain, sorrow, or joy he hears? Would he find relevance in what was said? Would he relate to the person's pain, sorrow, or joy?

The road to Emmaus story shows him doing all those things for his bereaved friends. When you view troubled participants with eyes of compassion, they experience the love of God and its healing power.

How do you help someone who constantly interrupts others?

As a facilitator, you try not to label participants, but it is important to note behavior. A season may come when a participant takes over the group by frequently interrupting others with lengthy comments about his or her own situation. The behavior may be rooted in enthusiasm, poor social skills, a lifelong character quirk, or lack of understanding of the ground rules of group process.

Confer with your partner to assess what is going on. Is the group bothered by the zealous participant or do they accept each other as they are and make light of disruptive behavior? If the latter is true, the disturbances usually disappear as the person gets comfortable with the group. On the other hand, when interruptions by a participant (let's call him "John") disrupt the flow of sharing, you need to act. If you don't, participants may resent "John," and confrontations occur. Sometimes meeker participants stop sharing or quit the group.

Review group etiquette, emphasizing taking turns and respectful listening. If a disruptive incident follows, I might

apply the rules by saying, "We appreciate your enthusiasm, John, but now it's Joan's turn to speak." Also be mindful of what triggers John's contributions. Eye contact with the facilitator is enough for some participants to start talking. To test that notion, choose a seat at the next session that keeps "John" out of your line of vision. It could solve the problem. Speak to your "John" privately about interrupting others if you need to. It's risky, but if it's done with respect and care for him plus openness to God's will, the disruptive behavior generally improves.

Does Seasons of Hope discuss Church issues?

Participants are not asked to debate or share opinions about topics such as theology, Church practices, or issues in the headlines. *Seasons of Hope* faith sharing focuses on Christ and the personal concerns of the bereaved. Scripture isn't dissected either. The word is proclaimed to open everyone to Christ, not to preach about how anyone should feel or act.

Do facilitators offer advice?

A facilitator is not an adviser, although it's tempting to give advice when asked. You certainly can share your experience with loss. But whatever eased your pain and grief may not be helpful for everyone. God will help others in different ways.

Through the faith sharing process you hope participants listen to the promptings of their own heart and soul. That is where God places his answers.

Do you follow up with participants between sessions?

Decide with your teammate(s) whether to minister by phone between sessions. Some teams like to call everyone. I contact participants who are having a "bad" week or are absent without

PART

ONE

notice. Sometimes a call of concern brings a person back the next week.

Encourage participants to support each other during the week. They can record contact information in the Network Directory of the *Participant Journal* booklet.

How can **facilitators** *keep from taking on too much?*

Ministering to the bereaved is a very rewarding experience, but it also takes physical, emotional, and spiritual energy. The compassion you so freely shower on those who mourn is essential for you as well. Be kind to yourself. Keep your sense of humor, especially when everything doesn't go as planned.

How do you minister without exhausting yourself? Three things are important:

- Set your priorities.
- Know your limits.
- Don't take on problems that don't belong to you.

That means you have to say "no" on occasion. Your choices will keep you in ministry or drive you from it.

Your calling asks you to do your best for the bereaved and to leave the rest to the Lord. He will heal the brokenhearted when they are ready. Try to keep your eyes on Christ through prayer, reflection, and an occasional spiritual retreat. Trust that he will give you what you need to minister. Besides spiritual stamina, his help often comes through supportive clergy and other parish pastoral staff members, teammates, and family who willingly journey with you.

Fellowship

How does fellowship fit into **Seasons of Hope?**

The Fellowship Finale that completes each session encourages the bereaved to socialize with each other and the ministry

team. Through mingling informally, participants get to know each other as neighbors and members of the greater community. Loneliness can be set aside while they relax, enjoy each other, and build the community of faith.

 What's next?

Now that you have explored the essence of faith sharing, facilitating, and the benefits of fellowship, the next chapter explains how to host your weekly sessions.

About Weekly Sessions

When you think of sessions as encounters with the Lord, preparation takes on new meaning. Jesus' friend Martha prepared a gathering in his honor, but she was too busy serving to enjoy his company (Lk 10:38–42). Jesus truly appreciated Martha's hospitality, but he reminded her that her sister Mary's focus on him was the better part. Like he befriended Martha and Mary, Jesus has befriended you. Because he consoles you in your grief, you can serve others who mourn. Let your preparation honor him.

To help you minister, the first part of this chapter explains how to plan for successful sessions. The second part helps the weekly process come alive and has an Activity Checklist (page 80) that the team can use to organize a session.

Planning Ahead (four weeks to one week before a season begins)

Most teams look at a season as a whole and then review the needs of individual sessions.

 What's a quick way to see a whole season?

Review the Sessions-at-a-Glance table in the appendix for the season you are preparing (these tables begin on page 181). It's a must-have for your planning meeting and will be helpful as you read the information that follows.

Look across a row for a session's title, theme, time allowed, scripture used, Christ-centered activity, and faith sharing highlights. Look down a column to see how the season handles one of those components. The Activity column, for example, has the scripture passage for each session, optional music, and what participants do to reflect on God.

 How are seasons alike?

Every season follows a familiar six-week pattern of sessions that use these titles:

1. Point of Departure
2. Path to Understanding
3. Obstacles on the Journey
4. Path to Inner Healing
5. Way of Suffering
6. Final Destination

From season to season, sessions are conducted in the same manner. You always welcome with prayer and opening comments, read scripture to guide activity and faith sharing, comment on group accomplishments, pray for the deceased, and host fellowship.

 How do seasons differ?

Each season offers fresh themes, scripture, and ways to find Christ. Compare the four Sessions-at-a-Glance tables in the appendix for details.

How does a theme fit in?

Drawn from scripture, a theme shows the focus of a session. It may address confusion, memories of loved ones, lost dreams, fear, hope, searching for joy and consolation, or another issue that conveys the universal nature of suffering and God's concern for those who mourn.

What about time allotments?

Since groups differ, the time suggested in the Sessions-at-a Glance tables is the minimum you can expect to spend. This gives some leeway to reach the weekly two-hour goal. As the weeks progress, the Opening shortens because less program information is covered. The Activity of each session offers personal time to reflect on scripture and paves the way for Faith Sharing, which lengthens somewhat during the season. Use a Footprint to pace the session.

What is a Footprint?

A Footprint is the blueprint for a weekly session. Not only does it help you plan a nurturing meeting environment, but its script gives the words to conduct the session if you should need them. The Sessions-at-a-Glance tables found in the appendix are outlines of the six Footprints of each season. Part II of the *Guidebook* (pages 89–177) contains the twenty-four Footprints. Refer to one of them as you read the rest of this chapter.

Do participants receive a Footprint?

No. Participants receive a *Participant Journal* booklet that has a Guidepost page for each session.

PART
ONE

 *What do you look at first to plan a season?*

Focus on Items Needed in the Footprints. Some items create a welcoming atmosphere while others bring Christ into focus. Then consider optional items. The Activity shows how options can be used in the different sessions. Decide with your teammate(s) whether to add them to the basic reflection activities.

Where do you find things from the Items Needed list?

Some items like a bell, a crucifix, and rosary beads are common to our homes, or you could borrow them from a parish ministry. For example, the religious education department probably has colored paper and markers to share. The liturgy committee might have extra Stations of the Cross booklets, incense, or a crown of thorns from an Easter pageant.

Each season has different needs. Give yourself enough time to gather the items, especially if you want to purchase or order something.

What items are used each week?

The bare essentials are music and a player, a focal point display, bibles, *Seasons of Hope Guidebook*s for the group facilitators, *Participant Journal* booklets, and boxes of tissues.

Why is music used before sessions?

Sacred melodies create a mood in which participants can put their worries aside. What better way to open hearts and minds to scripture and God's consolation? A variety of spiritual music is on audiotape or CD. (See the appendix.) If you or your teammate(s) don't have a music collection or a player, borrow from the music or youth ministry, or try your diocesan resource center.

 ## *What focal point display is suggested?*

To center participants on Jesus during prayer and reflection, try some votive candles beside an image of the Lord. For variety, you could show portraits from a book such as *His Face: Images of Christ in Art*, edited by Marion Wheeler. You might also use small sculptures or statues. As themes change, you could add a relevant sacred symbol. Just be certain to keep the image of Christ prominent.

 ## *How will bibles be used?*

Everyone at *Seasons of Hope* reads along when the scripture is proclaimed. At home, participants also review scripture passages during journal work. It's all right to have different versions of the Bible. Wording may vary somewhat, but the message comes through. Have bibles on hand for those who don't own one or forget to bring it to group. Borrow copies from the religious education department, a prayer or bible study group, or the parish library.

 ## *How is the* **Participant Journal** *used?*

Each participant uses a journal both during sessions and at home. Facilitators should have one to use during the session, too. The journal gives quick access to the *Seasons of Hope* Prayer and the Guidepost page where participants find the scripture citation and reflection activity. Also use the booklet to point out journal readings and exercises to do at home.

 *Is the chair arrangement for the session something to discuss a month in advance?*

Yes. Whatever decisions your team can make before the first session the better. Here are some options for placing chairs in the room.

1. Everyone is in a circle for opening remarks, scripture reading, the exercises, and faith sharing. Put the focal point display on a low table in the center of the chairs that so that everyone can see it.

   The facilitator sits with the group but could stand at a lectern to share opening statements and instructions from the Footprint in the *Guidebook*.

2. The group is at a table, preferably a round one so that everyone is in view and earshot and can see the focal point display. This works for a group of eight or fewer, including the team. If a huge conference table must be used, space the chairs evenly so that no one is isolated.

   A table makes handling booklets and drinks convenient, but it has a downside. Participants who get emotional or need to leave the group for a few moments often won't budge because backing away from the table calls attention to them.

3. The group moves as different phases of the session occur. As participants gather, chairs are in rows (parted at the middle, if desired) facing the focal point display and the lectern. After opening remarks, the scripture reading, and the meditation/written activity, the group forms an open circle that begins and ends at the focal point display.

Each approach works. I particularly like the third option because participants quietly focus on the Lord before literally facing the group for faith sharing. They have to work together to make a circle and, in the process, they stretch, chat and gain a new perspective on the gathering. Regrouping stirs up energy—a good place for faith sharing to begin.

🍂 If a parish facility will be used, is an inspection visit advised?

Yes. The best way to plot out the room for greeting, session activities, and fellowship is to make a team visit well before sessions begin. A diagram (floor plan) of the room may be available from the building manager, or draw one. Use it to sketch where you want a lectern, chairs, and tables for greeting, the focal point display, musical equipment, and refreshments. The appearance of the room will send a message: let it be one of hospitality.

If a custodian is available to prepare the room for sessions, discuss the diagram with him or her during the planning stage. While there, check out the room's furniture. Is enough available? What about a stand (lectern)? Are extension cords needed for electrical outlets? Does the kitchen have appliances to heat water and brew coffee? Is ice available? What about water pitchers, paper goods, utensils, linens, and other hospitality items?

🍂 Do you need to discuss hospitality plans for sessions?

It's wise to include hospitality on the meeting agenda. Start with materials for the welcome process. Then focus on how the team will greet participants. Once the details are decided, divide the tasks with your teammate(s) and keep the plan handy for the first session.

🍂 What materials do you need to welcome participants to sessions?

Basic items include "Welcome to *Seasons of Hope*" signs, a sign-in sheet, pencils, nametags and marking pens, and *Participant Journals*. If registration information isn't collected in advance by phone or mail, have forms that include the participant's contact data and the name and anniversary date of the deceased loved

one. If information is collected in advance, be sure to have extra forms for drop-ins.

If a welcome table will be used, discuss whether to add a tablecloth, welcome sign, and decorations of the season. Since participants like to know who is in charge, consider unique nametags for the ministry team.

For sessions at a home, what needs to be considered?

Decide how to greet participants. Will you post a "Welcome to *Seasons of Hope*" sign outside so participants know it's the place? Who will be at the front door? Who will register participants and handle questions? How will registration be handled?

For sessions at a parish facility, what needs to be considered?

Creating a welcoming atmosphere is equally important in the parish setting. Each week we put a "Welcome to *Seasons of Hope*" sign at the entrance. When long, winding corridors lead to the room, we mark the way for the first couple of weeks. Simple 8.5x11 sheets, hand printed or computer generated, serve the purpose. Just remember tacks or tape for posting.

A personal welcome at the entrance is ideal. If possible, station someone there thirty minutes before the session begins. Pick the most outgoing teammate with a ready smile and knack for putting people at ease. If a bereavement minister isn't available, ask a friend to lend a hand.

Is a welcome table necessary at a parish facility?

A welcome table is useful for the first week or two to greet and register participants, distribute *Participant Journals*, and assist latecomers. Thereafter, a greeter can handle the sign-in sheets

PART

ONE

(attendance and refreshments), offer nametags, and receive any donated refreshments for the session.

What about the refreshments?

Will the ministry have them? If so, will the team donate snacks or purchase them through the parish? Will one teammate take charge, or will it be a team effort? Will participants contribute? If so, will a signup sheet be used? What about reminder calls? How will contributions be acknowledged?

Also discuss the refreshment table. Where will it be? What will it offer during sessions? What will it offer during Fellowship Finale?

Could Fellowship be held before a session or at a break?

It could, but placing it last is recommended. Fellowship time lets participants get to know each other as neighbors and community members, but often something said during Faith Sharing touches another's heart. Placed last, Fellowship Finale gives participants a chance to talk privately about things that come up in group. They minister to each other—an important *Seasons of Hope* goal.

Teamwork for the Weekly Sessions

Once the program is planned, what's next?

The success of each session begins well before participants arrive. Discuss what each teammate will do the day of sessions. The following questions define roles.

What will the facilitator do on the day of the session?

The facilitator sets up and cleans the room with other members of the team. But don't get caught up in the work like Jesus' friend Martha did. As participants arrive, make them feel welcome. Guided by the Footprint, you move the session along at a reasonable pace.

What if a pastor or another parish staff professional is on the team?

If your pastor or other pastoral staff member is on the team, ask if he or she wants to facilitate with you. He or she might want to welcome everyone, introduce the team, lead prayer, and share in facilitating the group. Whatever this person contributes to Faith Sharing and Fellowship will enhance the group's journey together.

What will teammates do?

Teammates set up and clean up, distribute bibles, proclaim the Word, help with activities, facilitate or assist during Faith Sharing, take charge of refreshments, and mingle with participants during the Fellowship Finale. In other words, teamwork is why *Seasons of Hope* succeeds.

What happens just before each session?

When you and your teammates prepare the meeting place, also prepare yourselves. Pray together in Jesus' name and ask God to inspire you and those who come. The session Footprint lets you facilitate with confidence. The following offers additional tips on the process.

What are the unique traits of Seasons of Hope *meetings?*

Using the Footprints

1. Session Opening

 ### Who gets the session going?

The responsibility lies with the facilitator even when the pastor or another pastoral staff member is present. The facilitator cues this person and his or her teammates when they should step in to welcome, lead prayer, etc.

 ### What does the welcome involve?

The welcome reflects a spirit of hospitality and love for our brothers and sisters in Christ, many of whom are strangers. It takes courage for each person to come to the program. So acknowledge that bravery and let the participants know that the team is glad they came!

 ### How formal should team introductions be?

Each ministry team's personality comes out in the introductions. Decide what will be done. Will the team be together at a lectern or sit with the group? Will anything besides names be shared with participants? Even though some getting acquainted happens beforehand, be certain to formally introduce all team members.

 ### Does everyone recite the Seasons of Hope Prayer together?

Yes. Participants find it in the *Participant Journal*. Teammates use the *Journal* or *Guidebook*.

 *How are participant introductions handled?*

The Footprint offers guidance each week. Some people choke up in a new group and others feel compelled to talk at length. Neither way gets the first session off on the right foot. So ease into introductions by keeping it simple: their name and relation to the deceased. Assure participants that details get shared in a few minutes.

 *How do you present* **Seasons of Hope** *to the group?*

The Footprint makes it easy. What to say is written in the text. Or you could create your own presentation. Whatever you do include the Christ-centered goals, importance of fellowship, housekeeping concerns, and how to use the journal.

 *How do you know when to say what is written in the text?*

Throughout the Footprint an italicized heading—*Script*—indicates when to present the text that follows.

 *Are the stages of grief formally presented?*

No. *Seasons of Hope* emphasizes the spiritual side of mourning and finding consolation in Jesus Christ. Yet the stages of grief aren't ignored. They are revealed in the emotions and behaviors portrayed by participants who tell their stories.

For those interested in grief stages, the *Participant Journal* offers self-help resources. Participants are also invited to share bereavement works that help them.

 Is the home assignment in the **Participant Journal** *discussed?*

During the Opening from the second session onward, you ask participants their experience with a Church tradition or a work of mercy assigned in the Moving Forward section of the journal. The rest of their journaling remains private.

What does housekeeping involve?

Housekeeping refers to miscellaneous announcements that range from where to find the restrooms to schedule changes to alerting participants when someone needs transportation.

2. Session Activity

What happens during the Activity?

By using the Footprint approach, the weekly theme comes alive through commentary, scripture, and reflection activities for the individual. Some sessions include optional music to heighten the imagery of the scripture passage. The Activity opens a participant's heart to Jesus' message for him or her. Have participants turn to the Guidepost page when you give directions for exercises in the Activity section of each session.

Why do teammates proclaim the word?

Although participants are certainly capable, the team is ideal for proclaiming the scripture passages. It provides an opportunity to involve a teammate in a very specific way and helps ensure that the reading is well prepared and proclaimed. Additionally, participants don't have to worry about being called upon at random to read aloud for the whole group.

🌿 What if participants have never used a bible?

Thanks to Vatican II, many Catholics are now avid Bible readers, but not everyone is. If someone needs help finding the passage, give him or her a hand. Be sure everyone has ample time to locate the page before proceeding.

3. Faith Sharing

Chapter 3 gives a lengthy discussion on the fine art of facilitating a faith sharing group. Here are some additional practical concerns.

🌿 What about group etiquette?

Without ground rules, the Faith Sharing time becomes a free-for-all. Participants need to know what a facilitator does and what is expected of them. Have participants turn to the Guide to Group Etiquette on page 59 of the journal when you explain the rules. Return to that page each week if needed.

🌿 What do you do if a co-facilitator is unavailable?

You can facilitate a group solo if you have to, but ask a dependable participant to signal when it's ten minutes before the end of the session. This will help you finish on time.

4. Summary

Although this phase has the least amount of time allotted for it, it is important.

🍂 *What might you say about the accomplishments of a session?*

You might share an insight you gained from the session or challenge everyone to think of a discovery he or she made. Another approach is to give your impression of the group's journey together.

🍂 *Why make all the announcements?*

Never underestimate the power of invitation. Your enthusiasm encourages commitment to the next session, Fellowship Finale, and journaling each week.

🍂 *Do participants have the prayer used in the Summary?*

No. The facilitator, the pastor, or another pastoral staff member prays the prayer of thanksgiving aloud and asks participants to pray silently for the souls of their deceased loved ones.

5. Fellowship Finale

🍂 *How much time is allotted for the Fellowship Finale?*

The two-hour session includes thirty minutes to gather at the end for informal fellowship.

🍂 *What happens if the formal session runs overtime?*

Shorten the Fellowship Finale. With proper pacing, however, there is plenty of time. You could add about twenty minutes to an early phase and not affect the finale.

🍂 *Do participants stay for Fellowship Finale?*

They do when the team is enthused about mingling with them. It takes time for participants to reach out to each other. When they get comfortable, a sense of camaraderie and parish community evolves. Then Fellowship becomes something that no one will want to miss.

🍂 *Is there an easy way to remember all the details?*

The following checklist comes in handy. It sums up the weekly process described in this chapter.

Team Activity Checklist

Before the Session

____ Read the Footprint and scripture passage for the week.

____ Gather Items Needed (listed in the Footprint).

Day of the Session

One hour before Opening:

____ Meet at the location and pray together.

____ Set up chairs, tissue boxes, lectern (optional), welcome table, focal point display, music equipment, beverages/ refreshments, and signs.

Thirty minutes before Opening

____ Greet participants.

____ Help with sign-in and nametags (weekly).

____ Distribute *Participant Journals* (week one).

Five minutes before Opening

____ Join participants (a teammate stays at welcome table).

(During the Session, facilitator uses a Footprint to lead the group)

Opening: 5–20 minutes (changes weekly)

____ Welcome everyone, mentioning the session theme.
____ Introduce the team.
____ Lead *Seasons of Hope* Prayer using the journal.
____ Seek information on participants noted on the Footprint.
____ Give program details (weeks one and two).
____ Invite participants to share journal ritual, self-help tools/books/community resources (weeks two to six).
____ Share housekeeping details.

Activity: 15–35 minutes (changes weekly)

Facilitator

____ Present the script about the scripture passage.
____ Invite a teammate to read the scripture passage.
____ Complete the script that follows the reading.
____ Give activity instructions (participants refer to Guidepost in journal).

Teammate

____ Read scripture.
____ Assist with materials for activities.

Faith Sharing: 25–50 minutes (changes weekly)

Facilitator

____ Explain ground rules and etiquette of group (use journal).

____ Pose Footprint questions to the group and encourage faith sharing.

Teammate

____ Act as silent partner.

____ Share in group discussion, if desired.

Summary: 5 minutes (facilitator, pastor, or other pastoral staff member)

____ Summarize accomplishments of the day.

____ Remind participants to complete journal homework.

____ Tell the theme of the next session.

____ Invite everyone to Fellowship Finale.

____ Offer "Prayer to the Giver of Hope".

Fellowship Finale: 30 minutes (Team)

____ Socialize with participants.

____ Circulate refreshment signup sheet, if desired.

After the Session (Team)

____ Put the space back in order.

____ Discuss group dynamics.

____ Look forward to the next session.

 How do you get formal feedback on a season?

At the last session of a season, survey participants about their *Seasons of Hope* experience. Pose your own questions or use the Season Survey in each *journal* booklet (see chapter 5 and the *Participant Journal*). The survey can give tangible proof of how God blesses your efforts.

At this point, you have the general knowledge you need to conduct a *Seasons of Hope* session with a Footprint from Part II of the *Guidebook*. The next chapter focuses on the *Participant Journal*.

About the *Participant Journals*

*P*articipant Journal booklets are an integral part of *Seasons of Hope*. Each season has its own booklet for you and participants to use during sessions. With the *Journal's* home exercises, participants can independently keep their focus on the spiritual side of mourning. To help you explain the *Journal* to the group and use it to the fullest potential yourself, this chapter presents an overview and the specific components that compose all four booklets.

 Why are the **Participant Journals** *important?*

- The *Journals* save you time by combining session activities into convenient booklets so that you don't have to create or copy handouts.
- *Journals* empower participants. With a new booklet each season, they have details on weekly sessions at their fingertips plus resources on bereavement and group process. Home activity pages deepen their soul work by offering a fresh way to reflect on the scripture story of the week.
- The *Journal* continues what a session begins. Mourning becomes a sacred journey on which the bereaved sense God's compassion, mercy, and love in their struggles.

What does each Participant Journal *contain?*

- "Seasons of Hope Prayer"
- Welcome to *Participant Journal*
- Guidepost page for each session
- Journal for home use
- Helpful Resources
- Network Directory
- Guide to Group Etiquette
- Season Survey
- Acknowledgments

Where is **Seasons of Hope** *explained in the booklet?*

An introduction to *Seasons of Hope* and how to use the booklet is found in the section called Welcome to *Participant Journal*.

What part of the **Participant Journal** *is used every session?*

The *"Seasons of Hope* Prayer" and the Guidepost page are used at each session.

What does the Guidepost contain?

- The Guidepost announces each session's title, theme, and scripture reading. Since participants read along in their bibles at the session, many use the citation to locate the scripture passage before the session begins.
- Marking the Route describes the group activity for the session. You may want participants to read along in the journal as you give instructions. Also point out where to do a writing exercise or take notes.

- Encourage participants to check the Guidepost before coming each week. It occasionally mentions a special item to bring to the session: for example, rosary beads.

What are the components of the home exercises?

- **Looking Back** takes a closer look at the scripture passage presented in the group session and offers another point of view for the participant to contemplate.
- **A Prayer to Find the Way** seeks God's assistance with the grief process.
- **Steps Along the Path** uses narrative and exercises to tie the scripture passage into the participant's experience of loss.
- **The Reflection** segment focuses on feelings surrounding loss.
- **Journal Entry** encourages a participant to write his or her story. By putting into words what may go unspoken, a certain amount of emotional energy is released, opening the person to God's grace.
- **Moving Forward** recommends a Church ritual (familiar forms of prayer or contemplation) that will aid in the letting go process or asks for a particular act of compassion.
- **Closing Prayer** offers words of gratitude to God.

How do you follow up on home journaling without invading privacy?

During the session Opening, I simply ask the group whether the Moving Forward ritual brought comfort. This allows participants to share but keeps more personal matters private.

 When is the Network Directory introduced and used?

The first session each season is a great opportunity to talk about the Network Directory with your group. The page has space to record names, phone numbers, and e-mail addresses, making it easy for participants to interact outside of sessions. Most participants use the Fellowship Finale or time before a session to gather information. Reaching out to others for support is an important step on their journey.

 What is in Helpful Resources?

Helpful Resources has titles of bereavement books that bring spiritual nourishment through comforting prayer, meditations, and guides to find the way after losing someone special. For those with access to the Internet, a variety of helpful Web sites lead to bereavement information, organizations, and publications.

 What about the Guide to Group Etiquette?

The guide explains the duties of a facilitator and what is expected from group members. The behavior outlined is simply the Golden Rule with examples of basic courtesy. To begin Faith Sharing at sessions one and two, ask participants to open to the Guide to Group Etiquette and review the information. If your group has difficulty with courtesy, return to the guidelines each week and emphasize areas that could improve.

 How is the Season Survey used?

This tool helps participants think about their personal experience with *Seasons of Hope* and offers the team valuable feedback. The open-ended statements give plenty of room for expression. No one is asked to rate the program or the facilitators, but such

comments appear occasionally under the "I'd also like to say . . ." statement.

The survey can be completed at home or during the last session. Either way, collect them! We do the survey at the beginning of the final session so it isn't forgotten. Scissors may be needed to remove the survey from the booklet.

* The survey is also available online at www.avemariapress.com.

Do participants find the Journals *helpful?*

Our surveys show that participants like the *Journals*. Some were so enthused that they sent *Journal* pages to grief-stricken loved ones and friends who didn't have the benefit of our group. I was touched by both their compassion and their faith in the *Journal*.

When a former participant wrote to me about the *Journals*, I realized their healing power. She wrote, "My niece died recently, and I want to thank you for the *Seasons of Hope Journals*. They are a blessing. I've been going through them again and have received much comfort."

Do new Journals *need to be ordered each season?*

Yes. The *Journals* accompany a particular season, so order accordingly. The four *Participant Journals*-at-a-Glance tables in the appendix outline what to expect each season.

You are now ready to embark on the *Seasons of Hope* ministry. Part II follows with its four seasons of Footprints. May your journey with the bereaved bring you ever closer to the Lord.

PART
TWO

Session Footprints

SEASON
ONE

Session ONE
Point of Departure

Theme: For Whom Are You Looking?

 Items Needed:

- nametags
- marker
- sign-in sheet
- pre-session music/player
- signs
- focal point (image of Jesus, votive candles)
- bibles
- *Participant Journals*
- timer or watch
- bell (optional)
- refreshment signup sheet (optional)

1. Opening (20 minutes)

SEASON
ONE

- ❖ Welcome the group, introduce the team, and pray together the *"Seasons of Hope* Prayer" found at the beginning of the *Participant Journals.*
- ❖ Invite participants to say their name and relation to their deceased loved one. Give an example: "My name is (Donna), and I lost a (daughter)". Assure them that they will share more during the session.
- ❖ Use the script below to explain the *Seasons of Hope* program, *Participant Journals*, and any housekeeping details.

 Script

"Blessed are those who mourn," our Lord assured us, "for they will be comforted" (Mt 5:4). *Seasons of Hope* brings us together to share in God's love. The support of this community will enable you to give voice to your unique journey and take a step toward healing and spiritual growth.

You are an expert on your grief. We aren't here to teach you about its stages. You meet them on your journey. Instead, we will explore mourning through scripture, prayer, reflection, and faith sharing. We will help you focus on your relationship with the Lord and the many ways his Church offers consolation. Along the way, you will find Jesus in others who mourn and within your own heart.

We ask that you bring a bible each week. You will read a passage here and review it again at home. Does anyone need to borrow a bible now? (Have a teammate provide them.)

Please bring your *Participant Journal* booklet too. We use a Guidepost page each week. You will also have a home assignment in the journal that gives a fresh perspective on the weekly scripture reading. There's also space to write about your loss, and a tradition of the Church that can bring consolation.

The session officially concludes with what we call the Fellowship Finale. It's our informal time together to share refreshments and get to know each other as neighbors and community members.

Now for some housekeeping details:

❖ We start promptly each week, so please arrive early enough to sign in and get a nametag.

❖ If you can't make a session, please tell us the week before or call (give name and phone number.)

❖ Restrooms are located (offer directions).

❖ Beverages are available at the (indicate refreshment table). Help yourself.

❖ If you have a favorite book or article on bereavement, please feel free to bring it to show the group.

This week (give names) brought snacks for our Fellowship Finale. Let's give a round of applause and thank (her/him/them). (Optional: We need help with refreshments. At the finale, please sign up to bring one plate of snacks. Thank you.)

Are there any questions?

2. Activity (20 minutes)

 Script

Many of us become distraught when someone we love leaves this life. We're in good company. Even the Lord's close friends had difficulty dealing with his death! Let's turn to John 20:11–18 for an account of Mary Magdalene at the tomb. It gives a compelling view into grief and the confounding path it puts before us. (Have a teammate read the passage aloud while participants read along in their bibles.)

If Mary Magdalene, a faithful disciple who stood at the foot of the cross on Calvary, let grief blind her to the presence of the risen Jesus, perhaps our preoccupation with our deceased loved ones simply mimics her saintly approach to loss. The first step in

her healing was to embrace Jesus and then to share that fateful encounter with others.

Your presence here shows that you seek the Lord, too. The exercise we are about to do is one way you can share your faith story. Let's open the *Participant Journal* to the Guidepost for session one.

Exercise

 Script

In a cluster group, each of you will complete the activity statements in your own words. (Review if desired.)

- My name is _____.
- My departed loved one's name is _____.
- His/her death happened _____ weeks/months/ years ago.
- The cause of death was . . .
- When he/she died, I was at . . .
- My fondest memory of _____

Here's how a cluster group works:

1. Find two people you don't know well and form a group. (Continue when the groups are formed.)
2. Decide who speaks first, second, and last.
3. Each of you has four minutes to complete your assignment.
4. Because listening is such a crucial part of being a participant, please don't interrupt while others tell their story.
5. Change speakers when you hear the bell.

The first speaker's time begins now. (Signal speakers at four-minute intervals.)

(Continue after each person has had time to speak.) Now let's form a circle.

3. Faith Sharing (25 minutes)

 Script

Now that you've shared a little about your loved one, it's time for Faith Sharing. Before we begin, let's review the Guide to Group Etiquette found in the *Participant Journal*. (Review the guide.)

Questions (use all that time permits):

1. After your loss, did you experience any emotions like that of Mary Magdalene?
2. If not, what did you experience?
3. How was Christ present to you when your loved one died?

SEASON ONE

4. Summary (5 minutes)

❖ Comment on what the group accomplished today.
❖ Announce the next session: Path to Understanding: *Our Source of Consolation*.
❖ Encourage *Participant Journal* work at home.
❖ Invite everyone to the Fellowship Finale.
❖ Pray "Prayer to the Giver of Hope" (group listens and prays silently.)

> O Loving God,
> spirit of consolation and giver of hope,
> we thank you for the gift of your faithful people
> who join us today.
> We ask you to bless and keep them in your care.
> Let us also pray for the souls of our departed
> loved ones.
>
> (Pause so that the group may call these to mind.)

May perpetual light shine upon them and bring
eternal rest.
We ask this through Christ our Lord.
Amen.

5. Fellowship Finale (30 minutes)

SEASON
ONE

Session TWO
Path to Understanding

Theme: Our Source of Consolation

 Items Needed:

- nametags
- sign-in materials
- pre-session music/player
- focal point
- bibles
- *Participant Journal*
- pencils
- "My Yoke is Easy" by John Michael Talbot on *Master Collection V.I The Quiet Side* (CD #2) (optional)

1. Opening (20 minutes)

- ❖ Welcome the group and thank those who brought refreshments.
- ❖ Identify the team members and together pray the *"Seasons of Hope* Prayer."
- ❖ Have participants say their name and that of the deceased, and their relationship. Give an example: "My name is (Donna), and I lost (Erynne), my (daughter)."
- ❖ If newcomers are present, review the program and *Participant Journal.*
- ❖ Seek feedback on the first *Participant Journal* home assignment: lighting a candle.
- ❖ Ask if anyone brought a bereavement book or article to share and invite him or her to do so.

2. Activity (20 minutes)

 Script

For some, the path of mourning is a lonely journey. Many of us are expected to return to "normal" shortly after the loss of our loved one. We soon discover, however, that grief lingers and that healing has its own timetable. Our funeral rites tell us that God is with us in the midst of our suffering. Later, when the visible support of family and friends tapers off, it helps to remember that the love and consolation of Christ remain within our reach. Let's turn now to Matthew 11:28–30. (Have a teammate read the passage aloud while participants read along in their bibles.)

Jesus' words are worth pondering. He invites us to draw near to him as a way of coping with our burdens, but he never intrudes. We must go to him.

(Proceed with music and exercise or do only the exercise.)

Music Option: ("My Yoke Is Easy" or comparable selection)

 Script

So let's go to him now. Sit back, close your eyes, and settle in your mind an image of the Lord. Imagine that the voice of the singer belongs to Jesus.

Exercise (Provide pencils.)

 Script

Let's open the *Participant Journal* to the Guidepost for session two.

1. Approach Jesus through the written word by making a list of three things that make you weary during mourning.

2. Then jot down an example of when you sought and received Jesus' help with one of the burdens.

I'll signal when it's time to begin Faith Sharing.

3. Faith Sharing (35 minutes)

(If needed, highlight group etiquette and the roles of the facilitator and participants.)

Questions (use as many as time permits):

1. How did God lighten your burden around the time your loved one passed on?
2. If nothing comes to mind, for what help were you praying?
3. How has God eased your grief recently?

4. Summary (5 minutes)

❖ Comment on what the group accomplished today.
❖ Announce the next session: Obstacles on the Journey: *Shattered Dreams*.
❖ Encourage *Participant Journal* work at home.
❖ Invite everyone to the Fellowship Finale.
❖ Pray "Prayer to the Giver of Hope" (group listens and prays silently.)

> O Loving God,
> spirit of consolation and giver of hope,
> we thank you for the gift of your faithful people who join us today.
> We ask you to bless and keep them in your care.
> Let us also pray for the souls of our departed loved ones.
> (Pause so that the group may call these to mind.)
> May perpetual light shine upon them and bring eternal rest.

We ask this through Christ our Lord.
Amen.

5. Fellowship Finale (30 minutes)

Session THREE

Obstacles on the Journey

Theme: Shattered Dreams

 Items Needed:

- nametags
- sign-in materials
- pre-session music/player
- focal point
- bibles
- *Participant Journal*
- music: "Abba, Father" by Carey Landry on *Abba, Father: Prayer Songs of Rev. Carey Landry* (CD) (optional)

1. Opening (10 minutes)

- ❖ Welcome the group and thank those who brought refreshments.
- ❖ Pray together the *"Seasons of Hope Prayer."*
- ❖ Have participants state their name, the name of the deceased, their relationship, and when the loss occurred. Give an example: "My name is (Donna), and I lost (Erynne), my (daughter), (several months) ago."
- ❖ Seek feedback on the second *Participant Journal* home assignment: reaching out to someone.
- ❖ Ask if anyone brought a bereavement book or article to share and invite him or her to do so.

2. Activity (15 minutes)

 Script

Most of us don't understand what life without our loved one will be like before he or she dies. We learn quickly though. It might sink in at the moment of death or when the unthinkable message is delivered. Sometimes we become numb to what is happening, which cushions the time around the funeral so that we aren't paralyzed by grief. But, eventually, we realize that our hopes and dreams of a future with the deceased are gone—shattered like a precious piece of pottery that falls from its shelf.

Let's turn to Jeremiah 18:1–6. This prophetic passage from the Old Testament portrays God as the greatest of potters. (Have a teammate read the passage aloud while participants read along in their bibles.)

It's hard to imagine being a pliable clump of clay that God keeps molding into whatever he pleases. Does he want to form us anew as we face our shattered dreams? Let's consider that possibility over the next few minutes.

(Use music here or simply move to the exercise.)

Music option: ("Abba, Father" by Carey Landry)

 Script

While you listen to the music, place yourself in the hands of the Father.

Exercise

 Script

Now let's open the *Participant Journal* to the Guidepost for session three.

1. Think about a shattered dream related to your loved one that you would like to share with the group.
2. How might you honor the dream in the future?
3. If you wish, jot down your thoughts.

I will signal when it's time to begin Faith Sharing.

SEASON
ONE

3. Faith Sharing (40 minutes)

Questions (use as many as time permits):

1. What shattered dream would you like to share with us?
2. If a shattered dream doesn't come to mind, can you share a dream that was fulfilled?
3. How might you honor the dream now?

4. Summary (5 minutes)

❖ Comment on what the group accomplished today.
❖ Announce the next session: Path to Inner Healing: *Finding Joy.*
❖ Encourage *Participant Journal* work at home.
❖ Invite everyone to the Fellowship Finale.
❖ Pray "Prayer to the Giver of Hope" (group listens and prays silently)

> O loving God,
> spirit of consolation and giver of hope,
> we thank you for the gift of your faithful people who join us today.
> We ask you to bless and keep them in your care.
> Let us also pray for the souls of our departed loved ones.
> (Pause so that group members may call these to mind.)
> May perpetual light shine upon them and bring eternal rest.

We ask this through Christ our Lord.
Amen.

5. Fellowship Finale (30 minutes)

Session FOUR
The Path to Inner Healing

Theme: Finding Joy

 Items Needed:

- sign-in materials
- pre-session music/player
- focal point
- bibles
- *Participant Journal*
- pencils

1. Opening (10 minutes)

- ❖ Welcome the group and thank those who brought refreshments.
- ❖ Pray the *"Seasons of Hope* Prayer" together.
- ❖ Seek feedback on the third *Participant Journal* home assignment: spending time before the Blessed Sacrament.
- ❖ Ask if anyone brought a bereavement book or article to share and invite him or her to do so.

2. Activity (20 minutes)

 Script

Have you wondered whether joy will ever be yours again? It's a concern that often goes unspoken during mourning. Yes, life goes on, but you may feel half alive. Things that once made

SEASON
ONE

you happy may no longer bring a smile. You may feel empty. Maybe the future seems bleak. Then one day your pain is forgotten for a moment. The relief brings you hope, but when does grief become joy?

Our Lord addressed this very concern with his followers when his time with them was almost over. Let's turn to John 16:19–24 for the story.

(Have a teammate read the passage aloud while participants read along in their bibles.)

The Lord's words convey confidence that your grief will become joy. Our next exercise helps you think about that.

Let's open the *Participant Journal* to the Guidepost for session four.

1.   Consider what might help you find joy during bereavement, especially those things that didn't find a place in your prayers.
2.   Then write a letter to God in the space provided. Ask for whatever would rekindle your joy.

I will signal when it's time to begin Faith Sharing.

3. Faith Sharing (40 minutes)

Questions (use as many as time permits):

1.   What is the hardest part of the day since your loss?
2.   What helps you through "everyday" tough times?
3.   Can you share a ritual of faith you do to honor the memory of your loved one?

4. Summary (5 minutes)

Comment on what the group accomplished today.

❖   Announce the next session: Way of Suffering: *Way of the Cross*.
❖   Encourage *Participant Journal* work at home.

❖ Invite everyone to the Fellowship Finale.
❖ Pray "Prayer to the Giver of Hope" (group listens and prays silently.)

> O loving God,
> spirit of consolation and giver of hope,
> we thank you for the gift of your faithful people who join us today.
> We ask you to bless and keep them in your care.
> Let us also pray for the souls of our departed loved ones.
> (Pause so that group members may call these to mind.)
> May perpetual light shine upon them and bring eternal rest.
> We ask this through Christ our Lord.
> Amen.

5. Fellowship Finale (30 minutes)

SEASON
ONE

Session FIVE

Way of Suffering

Theme: The Way of the Cross

Items Needed:

- sign-in materials
- pre-session music/player
- focal point
- bibles
- *Participant Journal*
- Stations of the Cross or illustrated pamphlet
- music: *Chant* (CD) by the Benedictine Monks of Santo Domingo de Silos (optional)

1. Opening (5 minutes)

- ❖ Welcome the group and thank those who brought refreshments.
- ❖ Pray together the *"Seasons of Hope* Prayer."
- ❖ Seek feedback on the fourth *Participant Journal* home assignment: finding something to rejoice about.
- ❖ Ask if anyone brought a bereavement book or article to share and invite him or her to do so.

2. Activity (20 minutes)

 Script

If you wonder whether God understands our pain, consider what Jesus went through on the way to Calvary. The brutality he endured went far beyond the physical. Surely, his spirit suffered a beating that those who mourn can recognize.

Let's turn to Luke 23:13–56 to focus on what the Lord went through. (Have a teammate read the passage aloud while participants read along in their bibles.)

The Stations of the Cross capture the passion of Christ in pictures for us. We'll look at that tradition today. (Show Stations of the Cross by posted pictures, a visit to church, or a pamphlet you distribute. The *Participant Journal* lists the traditional fourteen stations and more information is available at avemariapress.com).

(Select music and the exercise or the exercise only.)

Music: (*Chant* CD or music for meditation.)

Exercise

 Script

1. For the next ten minutes, contemplate the stations.
2. Identify which station shows the kind of suffering or sorrow you currently experience.
3. Then open the *Participant Journal* to the Guidepost page for session five and jot down your thoughts.

I will signal when it's time to begin Faith Sharing.

3. Faith Sharing (45 minutes)

Questions (use as many as time permits):

1. Which station reminds you of your grief? Explain.

2. In what way could others help you carry your cross of grieving?
3. What other Church tradition helps you find meaning in mourning?

SEASON **ONE**

4. Summary (5 minutes)

❖ Comment on what the group accomplished today.
❖ Announce the last session: Final Destination: *Untie Him*.
❖ Ask participants to bring a framed photo of the deceased to the last session.
❖ Encourage *Participant Journal* work at home.
❖ Invite everyone to the Fellowship Finale.
❖ Pray "Prayer to the Giver of Hope" (group listens and prays silently).

> O loving God,
> spirit of consolation and giver of hope,
> we thank you for the gift of your faithful people who join us today.
> We ask you to bless and keep them in your care.
> Let us also pray for the souls of our departed loved ones.
> (Pause so that group members may call these to mind.)
> May perpetual light shine upon them and bring eternal rest.
> We ask this through Christ our Lord.
> Amen.

5. Fellowship Finale (30 minutes)

Session SIX
Final Destination

Theme: Untie Him

 Items Needed:

- sign-in materials
- pre-session music/player
- prayer table with focal point
- bibles
- *Participant Journal*
- pencils
- camera
- incense for *Participant Journal* assignment

1. Opening (5 minutes)

- ❖ Welcome the group and thank those who brought refreshments.
- ❖ Pray together the *"Seasons of Hope* Prayer."
- ❖ Seek feedback on the fifth *Participant Journal* home assignment: making the Sign of the Cross mindfully.
- ❖ Ask if anyone brought a bereavement book or article to share and invite him or her do so.

2. Activity (35 minutes)

(If the chairs are in rows, form a circle.)

 Script

Each week in session we honor our deceased loved ones with word and prayer. This week we go a step further by showing pictures of them to each other.

1. Introduce your loved one in the picture and tell why the photo or setting is a favorite of yours.
2. Then walk the circle and show us the picture.
3. When you're done, place the photo on the prayer table with our image of Jesus. This brief walk is a symbol of your journey with us these past weeks.

I'll show you what to do. (Demonstrate for the group with a photo of your deceased loved one.)

4. Have teammates also share from their place in the circle.

Over the weeks, we learned about your loved ones. Seeing their pictures helps us know them better. Thank you for sharing.

Scripture (10 minutes)

 Script

We go on living after our losses, but down deep we may still yearn for our loved ones. Certain events, the holidays, or places that remind us of the past may bring pain. People say the hurt eventually diminishes, but we may wonder if we'll ever feel whole again. When we seek Christ in the midst of sorrow, the scriptures can be great teachers.

Let's turn to John 11:1–44 to see how Jesus and his friends faced the death of Lazarus. (Have a teammate read the passage aloud while participants read along in their bibles.)

Now let's apply the story through Faith Sharing.

3. Faith Sharing (30 minutes)

Questions (use all that time allows):

1. Around the time your loved one died, how did the Lord respond to your call for help? Explain.
2. Do any ties with your loved one need to be untied?
3. Does the scripture passage remind you of losing your loved one? In what way?

4. Summary (10 minutes)

- ❖ Comment on group accomplishments this season and share future *Seasons of Hope* offerings.
- ❖ Have participants do the Season Survey from the *Participant Journal* (or reproduced from download at www.avemariapress.com) and collect the completed surveys.
- ❖ Encourage *Participant Journal* work at home. Provide incense, if desired.
- ❖ Invite everyone to the Fellowship Finale.
- ❖ Pray "Prayer to the Giver of Hope" (group listens and prays silently).

> O loving God,
> spirit of consolation and giver of hope,
> we thank you for the gift of your faithful people who join us today.
> We ask you to bless and keep them in your care.
> Let us also pray for the souls of our departed loved ones.
> (Pause so that group members may call these to mind.)
> May perpetual light shine upon them and bring eternal rest.
> We ask this through Christ our Lord.
> Amen.

- ❖ Take a group photograph.

5. Fellowship Finale (30 minutes)

SEASON TWO

Session ONE

Point of Departure

Theme: Remembering

 Items Needed:

- nametags
- markers
- sign-in sheet
- pre-session music/player
- signs
- focal point (image of Jesus and votive candles)
- bibles
- *Participant Journals*
- timer or watch
- bell (optional)
- refreshment signup sheet (optional)

1. Opening (20 minutes)

❖ Welcome the group, introduce the team, and together pray the "*Seasons of Hope* Prayer" found at the beginning of the *Participant Journal*.

❖ Invite participants to say their name and relation to their deceased loved one. Give an example: "My name is (Mary), and I lost my (husband)." Assure them that they will share more during the session.

❖ Use the Script below to explain the *Seasons of Hope* program, *Participant Journal*, and housekeeping details.

SEASON TWO

 Script

"Blessed are those who mourn," our Lord assured us, "for they will be comforted" (Mt 5:4). *Seasons of Hope* brings us together to share in God's love. The support of this community will enable you to give voice to your unique journey and take a step toward healing and spiritual growth.

You are an expert on your grief. We aren't here to teach you about its stages. You meet them on your journey. Instead, we will explore mourning through scripture, prayer, reflection, and faith sharing. We will help you focus on your relationship with the Lord and the many ways his Church offers consolation. Along the way you will find Christ in others who mourn and within your own heart.

We ask that you bring a bible each week. You will read a passage here and review it again at home. Does anyone need to borrow a bible now? (Have a teammate provide them.)

Please bring your *Participants Journal* booklet too. We use a Guidepost page each week. You will have a home assignment in the journal that gives a fresh perspective on the weekly scripture. There's also space to write about your loss, and a tradition of the Church that brings consolation.

The session officially concludes with what we call the Fellowship Finale. It's our informal time together to share refreshments and get to know each other as neighbors and community members.

Now for some housekeeping details:

- ❖ We start promptly each week, so please arrive early enough to sign in and get a nametag.
- ❖ If you can't make a session, please tell us the week before or call (give name and phone number).
- ❖ Restrooms are located (offer directions).
- ❖ Beverages are available at the refreshment table (point it out). Help yourself.
- ❖ If you have a favorite book or article on bereavement, please feel free to bring it to show the group.

This week (give name[s]) brought snacks for our Fellowship Finale. Let's give a round of applause. (Optional: We need help with refreshments. At the finale, please sign up to bring one plate of snacks. Thank you.)

Does anyone have any questions?

2. Activity (20 minutes)

 Script

The Lord taught about his death and resurrection before they happened. Nevertheless, the empty tomb came as a shock to his followers—both women and men. The scriptures reveal a variety of reactions that parallel what many of us experience when someone we love dies. Let's turn to Luke 24:1–12.

(Have a teammate read the passage aloud while participants read along in their bibles.)

The women who encountered the empty tomb of Christ had a profound story to tell. Unfailing faith in the Lord allowed them to accept that he was alive. The apostles didn't believe the women; in fact, Peter had to investigate the tomb himself. How fortunate we are that these disciples responded differently. It encourages us to embrace the unique reactions people have to losing a loved one.

The way you and I respond to loss stems, in part, from the way our families of origin reacted to death. Today's activity provides a walk down memory lane. Let's open the *Participant Journal* to the Guidepost for session one.

In a cluster group, each of you will complete the exercise statements in your own words: (Review if desired.)

- My name is _____.
- What I remember most about wakes and funerals when I was a child is . . .
- The thing my parent(s) did that impressed me is . . .
- The part God played in what I remember is . . .

SEASON
TWO

Here's how a cluster group works:

1. Find two people you don't know well and form a group. (Continue when the groups are formed.)
2. Decide who speaks first, second, and last.
3. Each of you has four minutes to complete your assignment.
4. Because listening is such a crucial part of being a participant, please don't interrupt while others tell their story.
5. Change speakers when I signal.

The first speaker's time begins now. (Signal speakers at four-minute intervals.)

(Continue after each person has had time to speak.) Now let's form a circle.

3. Faith Sharing (35 minutes)

 Script

Now that you've shared some of your story, it's time for Faith Sharing. Before we begin, let's review the Guide for Group Etiquette found in the *Participant Journal*. (Review the guide.)

Questions (use all that time allows):

1. After your loss, what were you feeling?
2. How was Christ present to you when your loved one died?
3. How does a visit to the gravesite help your grieving? Or does it?

4. Summary (5 minutes)

❖ Comment on what the group accomplished today.
❖ Announce the next session: Path to Understanding: *Seeking Consolation.*
❖ Encourage *Participant Journal* work at home.
❖ Invite everyone to the Fellowship Finale.
❖ Pray "Prayer to the Giver of Hope" (group listens and prays silently).

> O loving God,
> spirit of consolation and giver of hope,
> we thank you for the gift of your faithful people who join us today.
> We ask you to bless and keep them in your care.
> Let us also pray for the souls of our departed loved ones.
> (Pause so that group members may call these to mind.)
> May perpetual light shine upon them and bring eternal rest.
> We ask this through Christ our Lord.
> Amen.

5. Fellowship Finale (30 minutes)

SEASON

TWO

Session TWO
Path to Understanding

Theme: Seeking Consolation

 Items Needed:

- nametags
- sign-in materials
- pre-session music/player
- focal point
- bibles
- *Participant Journal*
- pencils
- optional music: "Song Over the Water" by Marty Haugen on *Anthology II: The Best of Marty Haugen* (CD) or "My Soul Thirsts" by Dan Schutte from *Lover of Us All: Liturgical Music* (CD), or a comparable selection

SEASON

TWO

1. Opening (15 minutes)

- ❖ Welcome the group and thank those who brought refreshments.
- ❖ Introduce the facilitators and pray the *"Seasons of Hope Prayer"* together.
- ❖ Have participants state their name and that of the deceased, and their relationship. Give an example: "My name is (Mary), and I lost (Joe), my (husband)."
- ❖ Review the program and the *Participant Journal* if newcomers are present.
- ❖ Seek feedback on the first *Participant Journal* home assignment: prayerfully placing a memento with the deceased's picture.

❖ Ask if anyone brought a bereavement book or article to share and invite him or her to do so.

2. Activity (20 minutes)

 Script

Moving forward with life after losing a loved one sometimes seems impossible. Grieving may leave us with a defeated attitude that can cripple the spirit. This is especially true if we withdraw from familiar people and activities that remind us of our loss. We may learn not to speak of our grief because others don't seem to understand. We may grieve alone even though well-meaning people surround us.

The truth is, we are never truly alone. Jesus understands suffering and wants to console us. In today's scripture, we witness his desire to heal a crippled man who can't seem to move on. Let's turn to John 5:1–9. (Have a teammate read the passage aloud while participants read along in their bibles.)

The passage reveals much about Jesus. He knows who is hurting. He seeks the person's wishes. His question about a cure must have seemed odd to the man since the water of the nearby pool was believed to have healing power.

We believe that water is a symbol of birth and rebirth, and Jesus is the "living water" (Jn 4:10). Today's passage reveals that on Jesus' word alone the crippled man was healed. The question for us is simple: do we want to be healed by Christ and move on with our lives?

(Proceed with music and the exercise or the exercise only.)

Music: ("Song Over the Water" or "My Soul Thirsts" or a comparable selection.)

Script

Let's go to him now. Sit back, close your eyes, and bring an image of the Lord to mind. Imagine his healing water flowing over you, washing away your sorrow and tears.

Exercise (Provide pencils.)

 Script

Another way to approach Jesus is through the written word. Open the *Participant Journal* to the Guidepost for session two. Take the next ten minutes to:

1. Write about what cripples you spiritually.
2. Let Jesus know whether you are ready to pick up the pieces of your life.

I will signal when it's time to begin Faith Sharing.

SEASON
TWO

3. Faith Sharing (35 minutes)

(If needed, highlight group etiquette and the roles of the facilitator and participants.)

Questions (use as many as time allows):

1. How have you noticed the Lord (or others) nudging you to "pick up your mat"?
2. How do you feel about moving forward?
3. What needs to be reborn in your life now?

4. Summary (5 minutes)

❖ Comment on what the group accomplished today.
❖ Announce the next session: Obstacles on the Journey: *Stumbling Blocks*.
❖ Encourage *Participant Journal* work at home.
❖ Invite everyone to the Fellowship Finale.

❖ Pray "Prayer to the Giver of Hope" (group listens and prays silently).

> O loving God,
> spirit of consolation and giver of hope,
> we thank you for the gift of your faithful people who join us today.
> We ask you to bless and keep them in your care.
> Let us also pray for the souls of our departed loved ones.
> (Pause so that group members may call these to mind.)
> May perpetual light shine upon them and bring eternal rest.
> We ask this through Christ our Lord.
> Amen.

5. Fellowship Finale (30 minutes)

SEASON
TWO

Session THREE
Obstacles on the Journey

Theme: Stumbling Blocks

 Items Needed:

- nametags
- sign-in materials
- pre-session music/player
- focal point
- bibles
- *Participant Journal*
- stones of various sizes, shapes, colors, and texture
- "Build Up" by John Michael Talbot on *The Regathering* (CD) (optional)

1. Opening (10 minutes)

- ❖ Welcome the group and thank those who brought refreshments.
- ❖ Pray the *"Seasons of Hope Prayer"* together.
- ❖ Have participants state their name, the name of the deceased, their relationship, and when the loss occurred. Give an example: "My name is (Mary), and I lost (Joe), my (husband), (a year ago)."
- ❖ Seek feedback on the second *Participant Journal* home assignment: thanking consolers.
- ❖ Ask if anyone brought a bereavement book or article to share and invite him or her to do so.

2. Activity (20 minutes) ·

 Script

When we lose a loved one, the change of seasons, holidays, or other reminders of the dearly departed can make us feel sad. Yet we know through the writings of the prophets of the Old Testament that God yearns to revive the hearts of those crushed in spirit. Let's turn to Isaiah 57:14–15 to hear words of consolation. (Have a teammate read the passage aloud while participants read along in their bibles.)

The passage speaks of God's loving concern for those who suffer a major loss in life. It says the obstacles (stumbling blocks) before us will be removed because we are God's people. We are supposed to build up God's kingdom by using these stumbling blocks. When grief is used for good, it gains meaning for us as well as other believers. Could it be that a crushed spirit stimulates spiritual growth?

(Proceed with music or exercise.)

Music: (If stones are unavailable, play "Build Up" on *The Regathering* CD.)

 Script

While you consider the stumbling blocks in your life, listen to a musical interpretation of today's scripture passage sung by John Michael Talbot.

Exercise (Provide stones.)

 Script

For this activity select a stone from the basket. Pick one that has the size, color, shape, or texture that represents the stumbling block you currently face on your journey through mourning.

(Continue once everyone has a stone.) Open the *Participant Journal* to the Guidepost for session three.

1. Use the next ten minutes to write. Describe your "real" stumbling block.
2. Explain to Jesus what the stone you selected tells you about your loss.

I will signal when it's time to begin Faith Sharing.

3. Faith Sharing (40 minutes)

Questions (use all that time permits):

1. Do certain things make you stumble or take a step backward on your grief journey?
2. Has the Lord removed any stumbling blocks for you? Give an example.
3. What stone on your path to healing needs to be removed?

4. Summary (5 minutes)

❖ Comment on what the group accomplished today.
❖ Announce the next session: Path to Inner Healing: *Living Hope.*
❖ Encourage *Participant Journal* work at home.
❖ Invite everyone to the Fellowship Finale.
❖ Pray "Prayer to the Giver of Hope" (group listens and prays silently).

> O loving God,
> spirit of consolation and giver of hope,
> we thank you for the gift of your faithful people
> who join us today.
> We ask you to bless and keep them in your care.
> Let us also pray for the souls of our departed
> loved ones.

(Pause so that group members may call these to mind.)
May perpetual light shine upon them and bring eternal rest.
We ask this through Christ our Lord.
Amen.

5. Fellowship Finale (30 minutes)

SEASON
TWO

Session FOUR
Path to Inner Healing

Theme: Living Hope

 Items Needed:

- sign-in materials
- pre-session music/player
- focal point
- bibles
- *Participant Journal*
- colored paper and markers
- glass bowl and water

1. Opening (10 minutes)

- ❖ Welcome the group and thank those who brought refreshments.
- ❖ Pray the *"Seasons of Hope* Prayer" together.
- ❖ Seek feedback on the third *Participant Journal* home assignment: blessing stones.
- ❖ Ask if anyone brought a bereavement book or article to share and invite him or her to do so.

2. Activity (15 minutes)

 Script

The greatest treasure we can possess is faith in God. The scripture of this session affirms what the faithful know first hand—that faith is subject to trials that test our belief in God. In the throes of grief, recognizing God's loving presence brings hope. Let's turn to 1 Peter 1:3–9. (Have a teammate read the passage aloud while participants read along in their bibles.)

Scripture reminds us that our hope stems from the resurrection of our Lord. Hope in salvation is his gift to us—a gift that is present even when losing a loved one leaves us downcast about the trials we face.

(Proceed with the exercise.)

Exercise (*Provide colored paper and markers.*)

 Script

Grieving colors our lives. This week's group exercise gives us one way to take charge today, instead of letting grief rule us.

1. Select a colored paper that symbolizes your grief. There is no correct color, just one that appeals to your imagination.
2. Label the paper: "My Grief."
3. If you like, name a specific trial on the paper or draw about it.
4. Then take your grief paper and make it smaller. Tear it, fold it, or crumple it. In some way, show your "grief" what you'd like to do with it.

(Pause while participants complete the process.)

5. Now hand your grief over to the Lord. One by one come to the prayer table and place what remains of your "grief" into the bowl of water that symbolizes Jesus' healing power.

(Pause until everyone finishes.)

Let's open the *Participant Journal* to the Guidepost for session four.

Take a few minutes to write a thank you note to the Lord for taking your "grief" from you.

I will signal when it's time to begin Faith Sharing.

3. Faith Sharing (45 minutes)

Questions (use all that time allows):

1. Has someone done something to bring hope into your mourning? Explain.
2. Our Catholic faith has many traditions that inspire hope. Can you share a specific practice you do to help yourself?
3. Is there a Church tradition that you do with your family or friends that helps you?

4. Summary (5 minutes)

SEASON TWO

Comment on what the group accomplished today.

❖ Announce the next session: Way of Suffering: *The Cross*.
❖ Ask participants to bring rosary beads next week.
❖ Encourage *Participant Journal* work at home.
❖ Invite everyone to the Fellowship Finale.
❖ Pray "Prayer to the Giver of Hope" (group listens and prays silently).

> O loving God,
> spirit of consolation and giver of hope,
> we thank you for the gift of your faithful people
> who join us today.
> We ask you to bless and keep them in your care.
> Let us also pray for the souls of our departed
> loved ones.
> (Pause so that group members may call these to
> mind.)
> May perpetual light shine upon them and bring
> eternal rest.
> We ask this through Christ our Lord.
> Amen.

5. Fellowship Finale (30 minutes)

Session FIVE
Way of Suffering

Theme: The Cross

 Items Needed:

SEASON
TWO

- sign-in materials
- pre-session music/player
- focal point
- bibles
- *Participant Journal*
- *Chant* (CD) by the Benedictine Monks of Santo Domingo de Silos (optional)
- rosary beads

1. Opening (5 minutes)

- ❖ Welcome the group and thank those who brought refreshments.
- ❖ Pray the *"Seasons of Hope Prayer"* together.
- ❖ Seek feedback on the fourth *Participant Journal* home assignment: reaching out to another.
- ❖ Ask if anyone brought a bereavement book or article to share and have him or her do so.

2. Activity (10 minutes)

 Script

The faithful who lose a loved one know that suffering is part of discipleship.

Let's turn to Luke 9:22–24 to see what the gospel teaches. (Have a teammate read the passage aloud while participants read along in their bibles.)

Our losses happen, but Jesus says we have a choice about how we handle them. We can bear our cross alone or share it with the Lord and let him set the pace for us. When he steers us to a *Seasons of Hope* group, we find consolation on our painful journey. Jesus does warn, however, that the road ahead will be difficult even with him as a guide.

(Proceed with music and exercise or the exercise alone.)

Music: (If background music is desired, play *Chant* CD or a comparable instrumental number.)

Exercise (Provide pencils.)

 Script

Let's open the *Participant Journal* to the Guidepost for session five. Today's exercise calls for rosary beads. Does everyone have a pair? (Provide rosaries as needed. A guide to the Rosary is available at avemariapress.com).)

1. The prayers of the rosary begin and end with the cross of Christ, so use the crucifix to silently reflect upon the suffering of our Savior.
2. If you like, jot down your thoughts.

Take about five minutes for the exercise. I will signal when it's time to begin Faith Sharing.

3. Faith Sharing (50 minutes)

Questions (use all that time permits):

1. You bear many crosses during mourning. Which cross in particular brings you close to the Lord? Explain why.
2. Which cross keeps you from the Lord? Why?
3. What part, if any, does praying the rosary or turning to the Blessed Mother play in coping with your grief?

SEASON

TWO

4. Summary (5 minutes)

- ❖ Comment on what the group accomplished today.
- ❖ Announce the next session: Final Destination: *Do Not Be Afraid*.
- ❖ Ask participants to bring an item next week that reminds them of their loved one.
- ❖ Encourage *Participant Journal* work at home.
- ❖ Invite everyone to the Fellowship Finale.
- ❖ Pray "Prayer to the Giver of Hope" (group listens and prays silently).

> O loving God,
> spirit of consolation and giver of hope,
> we thank you for the gift of your faithful people who join us today.
> We ask you to bless and keep them in your care.
> Let us also pray for the souls of our departed loved ones.
> (Pause so that group members may call these to mind.)
> May perpetual light shine upon them and bring eternal rest.
> We ask this through Christ our Lord.
> Amen.

5. Fellowship Finale (30 minutes)

Session SIX
Final Destination

Theme: Do Not Be Afraid

 Items Needed:

- sign-in materials
- pre-session music/player
- prayer table with focal point
- bibles
- *Participant Journal*
- pencils
- camera
- something that reminds you of your loved one

SEASON

TWO

1. Opening (5 minutes)

- ❖ Welcome the group and thank those who brought refreshments.
- ❖ Pray the *"Seasons of Hope* Prayer" together.
- ❖ Seek feedback on the fifth *Participant Journal* home assignment: contemplating the sorrowful mysteries.
- ❖ Ask if anyone brought a bereavement book or article to share and have him or her do so.

2. Activity (30 minutes)

(If chairs are in rows, have group form a circle.)

 Script

Each week in session we honor our deceased loved ones with word and prayer. This week we go a step further. You will each have a chance to:

1. Show something that reminds you of your loved one and tell why it is special.
2. Then place the item on the prayer table.

Who would like to go first? (Team shares last.)

Thank you for sharing. It's nice to know more about your loved ones. Now we'll focus on scripture.

Scripture

 Script

It seems that people of faith have a powerful advantage when death occurs. Let's turn to Luke 8:40–42 and 49–56 to learn what scripture has to say on the topic. (Have a teammate read the passage aloud while participants read along in their bibles.)

We can understand why the synagogue official sought Jesus for a dying child. Didn't we seek the Lord's help for our loved ones? We may have hoped for a miracle, but sometimes God wants our loved ones to have eternal rest.

In our grief, it helps to remember that nothing will stop the love of the Lord. The passage relates that Jesus had to work his way through a crowd that crushed in on him, but he rescued the child. Surely, your loved one also received his loving mercy. He is here for you, too.

3. Faith Sharing (35 minutes)

Questions (use all that time allows):

1. In what way did you invite Jesus into your life once you lost your loved one? If not, how might you?
2. Have any of your beliefs about God changed because of mourning? Explain.

4. Summary (10 minutes)

❖ Comment on group accomplishments this season.
❖ Share future *Seasons of Hope* offerings.
❖ Encourage the last *Participant Journal* work at home.
❖ Have participants do the Season Survey in the *Participant Journal* (or reproduced from the download at www.avemariapress.com) and collect them.
❖ Invite everyone to the Fellowship Finale.
❖ Pray "Prayer to the Giver of Hope" (group listens and prays silently).

> O loving God,
> spirit of consolation and giver of hope,
> we thank you for the gift of your faithful people who join us today.
> We ask you to bless and keep them in your care.
> Let us also pray for the souls of our departed loved ones.
> (Pause so that group members may call these to mind.)
> May perpetual light shine upon them and bring eternal rest.
> We ask this through Christ our Lord.
> Amen.

❖ Take a group photograph.

5. Fellowship Finale (30 minutes)

SEASON
THREE

Session ONE
Point of Departure

Theme: Believing

 Items Needed:

- nametags
- markers
- sign-in sheet
- pre-session music/player
- signs
- focal point (image of Jesus and votive candles)
- bibles
- *Participant Journal*
- timer or watch
- bell
- refreshment signup sheet (optional)

1. Opening (20 minutes)

❖ Welcome the group and introduce the team.
❖ Pray together the *"Seasons of Hope Prayer"* found at the beginning of the *Participant Journals.*

Point of Departure: *Believing*

❖ Invite participants to say their names and their relation to their deceased loved one. Give an example: "My name is (Jack), and I lost my (wife)." Assure them that they will share more during the session.

❖ Use the script below to explain the *Seasons of Hope* program, *Participant Journal*, and any housekeeping details.

 Script

"Blessed are those who mourn," our Lord assured us, "for they will be comforted" (Mt 5:4). *Seasons of Hope* brings us together to share in God's love. The support of this community will enable you to give voice to your unique journey and take a step toward healing and spiritual growth.

You are an expert on your grief. We aren't here to teach you about its stages. You meet them on your journey. Instead, we will explore mourning through scripture, prayer, reflection, and faith sharing. We will help you focus on your relationship with the Lord and the many ways his Church offers consolation. Along the way you will find Jesus in others who mourn and within your own heart.

We ask that you bring a bible each week. You will read a passage here and review it again at home. Does anyone need to borrow a bible now? (Have a teammate provide them.)

Please bring your *Participant Journal* booklet, too. We use a Guidepost page each week. You will have a home assignment in the journal that gives a fresh perspective on the weekly scripture. There's also space to write about your loss, and a tradition of the Church that brings consolation.

The session officially concludes with what we call the Fellowship Finale. It's our informal time together to share refreshments and get to know each other as neighbors and community members.

Now for some housekeeping details:

SEASON
THREE

❖ We start promptly each week, so arrive early enough to sign in and get a nametag.

❖ If you can't make a session, please tell us the week before or call (provide name and phone number).

❖ Restrooms are located (offer directions).

❖ Beverages are available at the refreshment table (point it out). Help yourself.

❖ If you have a favorite book or article on bereavement, feel free to bring it to show the group.

❖ This week,(give name[s]) brought snacks for fellowship. Let's give a round of applause. (Optional: We need help with refreshments. At the finale, please sign up to bring one plate of snacks. Thank you.)

Does anyone have any questions?

2. Activity (20 minutes)

 Script

We begin this new season with a close look at the reaction of the apostle Thomas to news that the crucified Jesus had been raised from the dead and appeared to the other disciples. Let's turn to John 20:24–29. (Have a teammate read the passage aloud while participants read along in their bibles.)

Thomas was not a person who would easily accept the word of others. He not only had to see the marks of the nails in Jesus' hands for himself, he insisted that he must also touch his wounds. The apostle's disbelief was profound. Yet how many of us who learn of someone's death are left in shock and disbelief?

The way you and I respond to news surrounding the loss of someone is rooted in our family of origin's ideas and rules about death and how to respond to it. Today's exercise visits the past.

Exercise

 Script

Let's open the *Participant Journal* to the Guidepost for session one. In a cluster group, you will complete the statements you find there: (Review if desired.)

- My name is _____.
- The rules about dealing with death that I remember from childhood are. . .
- The person who laid down the rules was . . .
- The rules taught me that God . . .

Here's how a cluster group works:

1. Find two people you don't know well and form a group.

(Continue when the groups are formed.)

2. Decide who will speak first, second, and last.
3. Each of you has four minutes to share your responses.
4. Because listening is such a crucial part of being a participant, please don't interrupt while others tell their story.
5. Change speakers when I signal.

SEASON
THREE

The first speaker's time begins now. (Signal speakers at four-minute intervals.)

(Continue after each person has had time to speak.) Now let's form a circle.

3. Faith Sharing (35 minutes)

 Script

Now that you've shared some of your story, it's time for Faith Sharing. Before we begin, let's review the Guide to Group Etiquette found in the *Participant Journal*. (Review the guide.)

Questions (use all that time permits):

1. As the scripture story shows, disbelief can accompany our losses. When did your loved one's death become real for you?
2. Do you still struggle to comprehend?
3. In what way has your faith in God influenced your grieving?

4. Summary (5 minutes)

❖ Comment on what the group accomplished today.
❖ Announce the next session: Path to Understanding: *Knock and the Door Shall Be Opened*
❖ Encourage *Participant Journal* work at home.
❖ Invite everyone to the Fellowship Finale.
❖ Pray "Prayer to the Giver of Hope" (group listens and prays silently).

> O loving God,
> spirit of consolation and giver of hope,
> we thank you for the gift of your faithful people who join us today.
> We ask you to bless and keep them in your care.
> Let us also pray for the souls of our departed loved ones.
> (Pause so that group members may call these to mind.)
> May perpetual light shine upon them and bring eternal rest.
> We ask this through Christ our Lord.
> Amen.

5. Fellowship Finale (30 minutes)

SEASON
THREE

Session TWO
Path to Understanding

Theme: Knock and the Door Shall Be Opened

 Items Needed:

- nametags
- sign-in materials
- pre-session music/player
- focal point
- bibles
- *Participant Journal*
- pencils/color markers

1. Opening (20 minutes)

- ❖ Welcome the group and thank those who brought refreshments.
- ❖ Identify team members and pray together the *"Seasons of Hope* Prayer."
- ❖ Have participants say their name, the name of the deceased, and their relationship. Give an example: "My name is (Jack), and I lost my (wife), (Linda)."
- ❖ If newcomers are present, review the program and the *Participant Journal.*
- ❖ Seek feedback on the first *Participant Journal* home assignment: visiting a gravesite.
- ❖ Ask if anyone brought a bereavement book or article to share and invite him or her to do so.

2. Activity (20 minutes)

 Script

The grief of losing a loved one can be emotionally and spiritually crippling if Jesus is not sought. His healing power is present for those who mourn but is never forced on anyone. When we pray, we spiritually knock on the door to God's heavenly kingdom. Let's turn to Matthew 7:7–11 to learn how to get a reply. (Have a teammate read the passage aloud while participants read along in their bibles.)

Jesus tells us to ask our heavenly Father for what we seek. When we ask in Jesus' name, it is as if we send him to do the knocking for us.

Exercise (Provide pencils/ markers.)

 Script

Jesus wants to be invited into your sorrow, so he will knock at your door. Since you are here, it seems that you already heard him knocking. When you open the door of your heart to him, you have taken the first step toward healing.

Let's open the *Participant Journal* to the Guidepost for session two.

1. Sketch Jesus at your door. If drawing isn't one of your talents, then conjure up the image in your mind's eye and write down a description of what you see.
2. Ask Jesus for something you want that will ease your grief.
3. Take about ten minutes for this.

I will signal when it's time to begin Faith Sharing.

SEASON THREE

3. Faith Sharing (35 minutes)

(If needed, highlight group etiquette and the roles of the facilitator and participants.)

Questions (use as many as time permits):

1. In what way has Jesus consoled you when you feel downhearted?
2. In what way has Jesus not consoled you when you feel downhearted?
3. Can you name a good thing God has given you recently?

4. Summary (5 minutes)

❖ Comment on what the group accomplished today.
❖ Announce the next session: Obstacles on the Journey: *Our Infirmities*.
❖ Encourage *Participant Journal* work at home.
❖ Invite everyone to the Fellowship Finale.
❖ Pray "Prayer to the Giver of Hope" (group listens and prays silently).

> O loving God,
> spirit of consolation and giver of hope,
> we thank you for the gift of your faithful people who join us today.
> We ask you to bless and keep them in your care.
> Let us also pray for the souls of our departed loved ones.
> (Pause so that group members may call these to mind.)
> May perpetual light shine upon them and bring eternal rest.
> We ask this through Christ our Lord.
> Amen.

5. Fellowship Finale (30 minutes)

SEASON

THREE

Session THREE
Obstacles on the Journey

Theme: Our Infirmities

 Items Needed:

- nametags
- sign-in materials
- pre-session music/player
- focal point
- bibles
- *Participant Journal*
- "You Raise Me Up" by Josh Groban on *Closer* (CD) or "We Will Rise" by John Michael and Terry Talbot on *No Longer Strangers* (CD) (optional)

1. Opening (15 minutes)

❖ Welcome the group and thank those who brought refreshments.
❖ Pray together the *"Seasons of Hope* Prayer."
❖ Have participants share their name, the name of the deceased, their relationship, and when the loss occurred. Give an example: "My name is (Jack), and I lost (Linda), my (wife), (six months) ago."
❖ Seek feedback on the second *Participant Journal* home assignment: prayerful knocking on the tabernacle door.
❖ Ask if anyone brought a bereavement book or article to share and have him or her do so.

SEASON
THREE

2. Activity (15 minutes)

 Script

What if Jesus stood before you and lifted the heavy burden of sorrow from you? What would you do? Let's turn to Luke 13:10–13 for a similar story from his day. (Have a teammate read the passage aloud while participants read along in their bibles.)

Like the woman who was unable to stand erect, we get weighed down by carrying the heavy burden of grief. Others saw the burden of her infirmity but only the Lord knew how to lighten her load. The exercise we are about to do brings Jesus' tender touch to the wounds of our grief.

(Proceed with music, exercise, or both)

Music: ("You Raise Me Up" or "We Will Rise")

 Script

Open yourself to the movement of the Holy Spirit while you listen to Josh Groban sing "You Raise Me Up" (or the Talbot brothers' rendition of "We will Rise").

Exercise

 Script

Let's open the *Participant Journal* to the Guidepost for session three.

1. Think about how it will feel when the Lord heals your wounded spirit.
2. Then jot down your thoughts.

I will signal when it's time to begin Faith Sharing.

SEASON

THREE

3. Faith Sharing (40 minutes)

Questions (use all that time allows):

1. What has weighed you down since you lost a loved one?
2. How has the Lord touched that weighed-down feeling? If he hasn't yet, what would you like him to do for you?
3. What do you do to ease that weighed-down feeling?

4. Summary (5 minutes)

SEASON **THREE**

- ❖ Comment on what the group accomplished today.
- ❖ Announce the next session: Path to Inner Healing: *Blinders to Faith*.
- ❖ Encourage *Participant Journal* work at home.
- ❖ Invite everyone to the Fellowship Finale.
- ❖ Pray "Prayer to the Giver of Hope" (group listens and prays silently).

> O loving God,
> spirit of consolation and giver of hope,
> we thank you for the gift of your faithful people who join us today.
> We ask you to bless and keep them in your care.
> Let us also pray for the souls of our departed loved ones.
> (Pause so that group members may call these to mind.)
> May perpetual light shine upon them and bring eternal rest.
> We ask this through Christ our Lord.
> Amen.

5. Fellowship Finale (30 minutes)

Session FOUR
Path to Inner Healing

Theme: Blinders to Faith

 Items Needed:

- sign-in materials
- pre-session music/player
- focal point
- bibles
- *Participant Journal*
- pencils

SEASON

THREE

1. Opening (10 minutes)

❖ Welcome the group and thank those who brought refreshments.
❖ Pray together the *"Seasons of Hope Prayer."*
❖ Seek feedback on the third *Participant Journal* home assignment: celebrating the sacrament of forgiveness.
❖ Ask if anyone brought a bereavement book or article to share and invite him or her to do so.

2. Activity (20 minutes)

 Script

Some who mourn don't even consider calling upon Jesus to ease their suffering. Scripture, however, highlights unique individuals who publicly seek the Lord's endless mercy and compassion. Let's turn to Luke 18:35–43 for one man's story. (Have a teammate read the passage aloud while participants read along in their bibles.)

The beggar who seeks sight is much like the grief-stricken who yearn for insight into their own predicament. Each situation demands trust in God.

Exercise (Provide pencils.)

 Script

Let's open the *Participant Journal* to the Guidepost for session four.

1. Think about the scene from scripture and what strikes you most about the story.
2. Take about ten minutes to write a letter to God. Ask him for something that will help you get through the grieving process.

I will signal when it's time to begin Faith Sharing.

SEASON
THREE

3. Faith Sharing (40 minutes)

Questions (use all that time allows):

1. Is your image of the Lord the same or different since losing your loved one?
2. Have you encountered a sacrament or a sacred tradition that helps you see the Lord more clearly now?
3. Others rebuked the blind man when he sought the Lord's help, yet he persisted. What lesson have you learned on your grief journey?

4. Summary (5 minutes)

❖ Comment on what the group accomplished today.
❖ Announce the next session: Way of Suffering: *His Wounds*.
❖ Encourage *Participant Journal* work at home.
❖ Invite everyone to the Fellowship Finale.
❖ Pray "Prayer to the Giver of Hope" (group listens and prays silently).

> O loving God,
> spirit of consolation and giver of hope,
> we thank you for the gift of your faithful people
> who join us today.
> We ask you to bless and keep them in your care.
> Let us also pray for the souls of our departed
> loved ones.
> (Pause so that group members may call these to
> mind.)
> May perpetual light shine upon them and bring
> eternal rest.
> We ask this through Christ our Lord.
> Amen.

SEASON

THREE

5. Fellowship Finale (30 minutes)

Session FIVE
Way of Suffering

Theme: His Wounds

 Items Needed:

- sign-in materials
- pre-session music/player
- focal point (crucifix or picture of Christ crucified)
- bibles
- *Participant Journal*
- *Maundy Thursday: Gregorian Chant* (CD) by the Monastic Choir of St. Peter's Abbey or an instrumental selection (optional)

SEASON
THREE

1. Opening (10 minutes)

- ❖ Welcome the group and thank those who brought refreshments.
- ❖ Pray together the *"Seasons of Hope Prayer."*
- ❖ Seek feedback on the fourth *Participant Journal* home assignment: helping someone who needs compassion.
- ❖ Ask if anyone brought a bereavement book or article to share and invite him or her to do so.

2. Activity (15 minutes)

 Script

Jesus, the guardian of souls, suffered because of his infinite love for us, and by his wounds humanity is healed. Yet the sorrow of losing a loved one can make us feel incomplete. When we focus on Jesus crucified, new meaning can come to our own loss and suffering. Let's turn to 1 Peter 2:20b–24 to focus on Christ. (Have a teammate read the passage aloud while participants read along in their bibles.)

Today's exercise will help you ponder Jesus' final hours.

(Continue with music and exercise or with the exercise alone.)

Music: (*Maundy Thursday* or an instrumental selection.)

 Script

SEASON

THREE

Gregorian chant is sacred music from the Church of the Middle Ages. It features rhythmic, unaccompanied monotone singing of the liturgy that alternates between soloist and monastic choir. As the music washes over you, contemplate the wounds of Christ crucified.

Exercise (Provide pencils.)

 Script

Open the *Participant Journal* to the Guidepost for session five.

1. Observe the wounds of Christ on display. Think about their meaning for you during mourning.
2. Write what comes to mind.

I will signal when it's time to begin Faith Sharing.

3. Faith Sharing (45 minutes)

Questions (use all that time allows):

1. During the passion, Jesus' surely must have suffered in mind and spirit. Can you tell us how suffering your loss makes you feel?
2. What helps lift your spirit?
3. How does being a disciple of Christ affect the meaning of suffering for you?

4. Summary (5 minutes)

SEASON THREE

❖ Comment on what the group accomplished today.
❖ Announce the last session: Final Destination: *Do Not Weep*.
❖ Ask participants to bring something next week that reminds them of their loved one's faith.
❖ Encourage *Participant Journal* work at home.
❖ Invite everyone to the Fellowship Finale.
❖ Pray "Prayer to the Giver of Hope" (group listens and prays silently).

> O Loving God,
> spirit of consolation and giver of hope,
> we thank you for the gift of your faithful people who join us today.
> We ask you to bless and keep them in your care.
> Let us also pray for the souls of our departed loved ones.
> (Pause so that group members may call these to mind.)
> May perpetual light shine upon them and bring eternal rest.
> We ask this through Christ our Lord.
> Amen.

5. Fellowship Finale (30 minutes)

Session SIX
Final Destination

Theme: Do Not Weep

 Items Needed:

- pre-session music/player
- prayer table with focal point
- bibles
- *Participant Journal*
- pencils
- camera
- a reminder of the faith of your loved one

SEASON

THREE

1. Opening (5 minutes)

❖ Welcome the group and thank those who brought refreshments.
❖ Pray together the *"Seasons of Hope Prayer."*
❖ Seek feedback on the fifth *Participant Journal* home assignment: receiving the Eucharist.
❖ Ask if anyone brought a bereavement book or article to share and invite him or her to do so.

2. Activity (35 minutes)

(If the chairs are in rows, form a circle.)

Script

Each week in session, we honor our deceased loved ones with word and prayer. This week we go a step further.

1. I invite each of you to show something that reminds you of the faith of your departed loved one and tell why it is special to you.
2. Then place the item on the prayer table.

Who would like to go first? (Team shares last.)

Thank you for sharing. It's nice to know more about your loved ones. Now we'll focus on scripture.

Script

The love Jesus brings to our lives through our loved ones may not be memorialized in great works like the Bible, but we take comfort in listening to its accounts of his divine kindness to those who mourn. Let's turn to Luke 7:11–17 for such a story. (Have a teammate read the passage aloud while participants read along in their bibles.)

Jesus didn't wait for the grieving widow to seek his help, but rather he reached out to her in love. Those of us who desire his compassion surely will not be disappointed.

3. Faith Sharing (40 minutes)

Questions (use all that time allows):

1. In what way does Jesus dry your tears of sorrow? If your grief isn't filled with sorrow, how has he helped you?
2. In what way would you like Jesus to show his compassion?

4. Summary (5 minutes)

- ❖ Comment on group accomplishments this season and announce future *Seasons of Hope* offerings.
- ❖ Encourage the last *Participant Journal* work at home.
- ❖ Have participants complete the Season Survey in the *Participant Journal* (or reproduced from the download at www.avemariapress.com) and collect them.
- ❖ Invite everyone to the Fellowship Finale.
- ❖ Pray "Prayer to the Giver of Hope" (group listens and prays silently).

> O Loving God,
> spirit of consolation and giver of hope,
> we thank you for the gift of your faithful people who join us today.
> We ask you to bless and keep them in your care.
> Let us also pray for the souls of our departed loved ones.
> (Pause so that group members may call these to mind.)
> May perpetual light shine upon them and bring eternal rest.
> We ask this through Christ our Lord.
> Amen.

Take a group photograph.

5. Fellowship Finale (30 minutes)

SEASON

THREE

SEASON
FOUR

Session ONE
Point of Departure

Theme: Last Encounter

 Items Needed:

- nametags
- markers
- sign-in sheet
- pre-session music/player
- signs
- focal point (image of Jesus and votive candles)
- bibles
- *Participant Journals*
- timer or watch
- bell (optional)
- refreshment signup sheet (optional)

1. Opening (20 minutes)

❖ Welcome the group, introduce the team, and pray together the *"Seasons of Hope* Prayer."
❖ Invite participants to share their names and their relationship to the deceased loved on. Give an example:

"My name is (Helen), and I lost my (sister)." Assure them that they will share more during the session.

❖ Use the script below to explain the *Seasons of Hope* program, *Participant Journal*, and any housekeeping details.

 ### *Script*

"Blessed are those who mourn," our Lord assured us, "for they will be comforted" (Mt 5:4). *Seasons of Hope* brings us together to share in God's love. The support of this community will enable you to give voice to your unique journey and take a step toward healing and spiritual growth.

You are an expert on your grief. We aren't here to teach you about its stages. You meet them on your journey. Instead, we will explore mourning through scripture, prayer, reflection, and faith sharing. We will help you focus on your relationship with the Lord and the many ways his Church offers consolation. Along the way you will find Jesus in others who mourn and within your own heart.

We ask that you bring a bible each week. You will read a passage here and review it again at home. Does anyone need to borrow a bible now? (Have a teammate provide them.)

Please bring your *Participant Journal* booklet, too. We use a Guidepost page each week. You will also have a home assignment in the journal that gives a fresh perspective on the weekly scripture. There's also space to write about your loss, and a tradition of the Church that brings consolation.

The session officially concludes with what we call the Fellowship Finale. It's our informal time together to share refreshments and get to know each other as neighbors and community members.

Now for some housekeeping details

❖ We start promptly each week, so please arrive with enough time to sign in and get a nametag.

SEASON
FOUR

❖ If you can't make a session, please tell us the week before or call (give name and phone number).

❖ Restrooms are located (offer directions).

❖ Beverages are available at the refreshment table (point it out). Help yourself.

❖ If you have a favorite book or article on bereavement, please feel free to bring it and show the group.

❖ This week (give name[s]) brought snacks for fellowship. Let's give a round of applause. (Optional: We need help with refreshments. At the finale, please sign up to bring one plate of snacks. Thank you.)

Does anyone have any questions?

2. Activity (20 minutes)

 Script

SEASON **FOUR**

When our departed loved ones are still with us, it is impossible to imagine life without them. Questions about eternal life also arise. At the last Passover meal, the disciples faced the same concerns when Jesus spoke about leaving them behind. Let's turn to John 14:1–8 to hear what transpired. (Have a teammate read the passage aloud while participants read along in their bibles.)

The dismay Thomas shared with the Lord opens the door for Philip, another disciple, to share his concerns about losing Jesus. Questions about eternal life concern all of us—sometimes quite intensely as when a loved one dies. Our views about what happens when someone dies start forming when we are children. The next exercise lets you share what your parents/ family did to ease their grief.

Point of Departure: *Last Encounter*

Exercise

 Script

Let's open the *Participant Journal* to the Guidepost for session one. In a cluster group, you will complete the activity statements you find there. (Review if desired.)

My name is _____.
The things my family did to ease grief were . . .
When I was sad over losing someone dear, I would . . .
In sad times, my family taught me that God was . . .

Here's how a cluster group works:

1. Find two people you don't know well and form a group. (Continue when the groups are formed.)
2. Decide who speaks first, second, and last.
3. Each of you has four minutes to complete your assignment.
4. Please don't interrupt while others tell their story. Listening is an important part of being a participant.
5. Change speakers when I signal.

The first speaker's time begins now. (Signal speakers at four-minute intervals.)

(Continue after each person has had time to speak.) Now let's form a circle.

SEASON
FOUR

3. Faith Sharing (35 minutes)

 Script

Now that you've shared some of your story, it's time for Faith Sharing. Before we begin, let's review the Guide for Group Etiquette found in the *Participant Journal*.

Questions (use all that time allows):

1. Jesus wanted the disciples to have faith and not worry. What role has worry played in mourning your loved one?
2. In what way does believing in God influence the way you cope with being left behind?
3. Has your loss made you think about the dwelling place God the Father has for you in his house?

4. Summary (5 minutes)

❖ Comment on what the group accomplished today.
❖ Announce the next session: Path to Understanding: *The Garden of Gethsemane.*
❖ Encourage *Participant Journal* work at home.
❖ Invite everyone to the Fellowship Finale.
❖ Pray "Prayer to the Giver of Hope" (group listens and prays silently).

> O loving God,
> spirit of consolation and giver of hope,
> we thank you for the gift of your faithful people
> who join us today.
> We ask you to bless and keep them in your care.
> Let us also pray for the souls of our departed
> loved ones.
> (Pause so that group members may call these to
> mind.)
> May perpetual light shine upon them and bring
> eternal rest.
> We ask this through Christ our Lord.
> Amen.

5. Fellowship Finale (30 minutes)

SEASON
FOUR

Session TWO
Path to Understanding

Theme: The Garden of Gethsemane

 Items Needed:

- nametags
- markers
- sign-in sheet
- pre-session music/player
- focal point
- bibles
- *Participant Journal*
- pencils

1. Opening (20 minutes)

- ❖ Welcome the group and thank those who brought refreshments.
- ❖ Introduce the team members and pray together the *"Seasons of Hope* Prayer."
- ❖ Have participants share their name, that of the deceased, and their relationship. Give an example: "My name is (Helen), and I lost (Kate), my (sister)."
- ❖ If newcomers are present, review the program and *Participant Journal.*
- ❖ Seek feedback on the first *Participant Journal* home assignment: centering prayer.
- ❖ Ask if anyone brought a bereavement book or article to share and invite him or her to do so.

SEASON

FOUR

2. Activity (15 minutes)

 Script

Mourning can trouble us deeply, bringing great sorrow to our hearts. When we feel betrayed and alone in our grief, we are not far from the agony Jesus suffered in the Garden of Gethsemane. Let's turn to Mark 14:32–42 to listen carefully to our Lord's ordeal. (Have a teammate read the passage aloud while participants read along in their bibles.)

The remarkable scene in the garden reveals Jesus' way of coping. He prayed fervently to the Father as he struggled with what was to come; yet, he desired above all else to fulfill the Father's will. The cup of suffering passes to his disciples today and tests even the most devout among us.

Exercise (Provide pencils.)

 Script

Let's open the Participant Journal to the Guidepost for session two.

1. During the next ten minutes, imagine being in the garden where Jesus liked to pray.
2. Consider how the Father could help you in your time of distress.
3. Make a list of your requests in the *Participant Journal.*
4. I will signal when it's time to begin Faith Sharing.

3. Faith Sharing (35 minutes)

(Review group etiquette and highlight the facilitator and participant roles.)

Questions (use all that time allows):

SEASON
FOUR

1. If God answered one prayer that would ease your grief right now, what would it be? Explain.
2. Has your approach to prayer stayed the same or changed since your loss? Explain.
3. Do you have a friend like Peter, James, or John for support? Whether you do or not, what could someone do to ease your grief?

4. Summary (5 minutes)

❖ Comment on what the group accomplished today.
❖ Announce the next session: Obstacles on the Journey: *Crown of Thorns*.
❖ Encourage *Participant Journal* work at home.
❖ Invite everyone to the Fellowship Finale.
❖ Pray "Prayer to the Giver of Hope" (group listens and prays silently).

> O loving God,
> spirit of consolation and giver of hope,
> we thank you for the gift of your faithful people who join us today.
> We ask you to bless and keep them in your care.
> Let us also pray for the souls of our departed loved ones.
> (Pause so that group members may call these to mind.)
> May perpetual light shine upon them and bring eternal rest.
> We ask this through Christ our Lord.
> Amen.

5. Fellowship Finale (30 minutes)

SEASON

FOUR

Session THREE
Obstacles on the Journey

Theme: Crown of Thorns

 Items Needed:

- nametags
- markers
- sign-in sheet
- pre-session music/player
- focal point
- bibles
- *Participant Journal*
- a rose with thorns (and/or a crown of thorns, perhaps from an Easter pageant)

1. Opening (15 minutes)

SEASON FOUR

- ❖ Welcome the group and thank those who brought refreshments.
- ❖ Pray together the *"Seasons of Hope Prayer."*
- ❖ Have participants state their name, the name of the deceased, their relationship, and when the loss occurred. Give an example: "My name is (Helen), and I lost (Kate), my (sister), (last November)."
- ❖ Seek feedback on the second *Participant Journal* home assignment: genuflecting mindfully.
- ❖ Ask if anyone brought a bereavement book or article to share and ask him or her to do so.

2. Activity (15 minutes)

 Script

It is hard to fathom the human cruelty and pain Jesus experienced at the hands of his enemies. Some movies picture it for us, but a symbol of the passion such as the crown of thorns can also help us imagine the Lord's suffering of mind, body, and soul. Let's turn to John 19:1–3. (Have a teammate read the passage aloud while participants read along in their bibles.)

Grieving may not brutalize the body, but it does impact both our physical and mental health. Grieving also clearly affects the health of our souls. Spiritually speaking, our suffering unites us more closely to Jesus.

Exercise (Provide Pencils)

 Script

The thorns used in the crown to torture Jesus were probably from a thorn-plant not common to our world. But most of us can relate to prickly thorns found on a rose bush. The rose is another popular symbol in Christianity. Because it is a perfect flower, it is an image of wisdom and a symbol of Christ. With that in mind, let's turn to the *Participant Journal* for the Guidepost for session three.

1. During the quiet of the next few minutes, reflect on the pain of mind and spirit that Jesus endured for us. Let the thorny rose (or crown of thorns) on the table launch your thoughts.
2. Then write to Jesus about how you deal with the emotional or spiritual pain of your grief.

I will signal when it's time to begin Faith Sharing.

SEASON FOUR

3. Faith Sharing (45 minutes)

Questions (use all that time allows):

1. When you think of your grief, what is the most painful part—the biggest thorn?
2. When have found or might you find Jesus (the rose) among the thorns? Give an example.
3. Have you felt any easing of your pain recently? Explain.

4. Summary (5 minutes)

❖ Comment on what the group accomplished today.
❖ Announce the next session: Path to Inner Healing: *Gift of Caring*.
❖ Encourage *Participant Journal* work at home.
❖ Invite everyone to the Fellowship Finale.
❖ Pray the "Prayer to the Giver of Hope" (group listens and prays silently).

> O loving God,
> spirit of consolation and giver of hope,
> we thank you for the gift of your faithful people who join us today.
> We ask you to bless and keep them in your care.
> Let us also pray for the souls of our departed loved ones.
> (Pause so that group members may call these to mind.)
> May perpetual light shine upon them and bring eternal rest.
> We ask this through Christ our Lord.
> Amen.

SEASON FOUR

5. Fellowship Finale (30 minutes)

Session FOUR
Path to Inner Healing

Theme: Gift of Caring

 Items Needed:

- markers
- sign-in sheet
- pre-session music/player
- focal point
- bibles
- *Participant Journal*
- pencils

1. Opening (15 minutes)

- ❖ Welcome the group and thank those who brought refreshments.
- ❖ Pray together the *"Seasons of Hope* Prayer."
- ❖ Seek feedback on the third *Participant Journal* home assignment: receiving communion from the cup.
- ❖ Ask if anyone brought a bereavement book or article to share and invite him or her to do so.

2. Activity (20 minutes)

 Script

You know who your friends are when misfortune befalls you. At the end of Jesus' journey, only the youngest apostle, John, joined Mother Mary and the faithful women disciples

who stood at the foot of the cross. Let's turn to John 19:25–30 for the details. (Have a teammate read the passage aloud while participants read along in their bibles.)

In that era, a poor widow would have had a hard life if she did not have a child to support her. No wonder Jesus wanted his mother to have his disciple John as a son. Jesus cared about her welfare, but he also had a message for his followers: the Blessed Virgin Mary was to be mother to all God's children, and, like John, we are to care for others in his name.

Exercise

 Script

Let's open the *Participant Journal* to the Guidepost for session four.

1. In the space provided, write a letter to Jesus. Let him know who has stood by you. Express your gratitude for the gift of their concern and their acts of kindness.
2. If no one comes to mind, write about his gift of *Seasons of Hope*.

I will signal when it's time to begin Faith Sharing.

SEASON
FOUR

3. Faith Sharing (40 minutes)

Jesus had unfinished business on his mind during the last moments of his life. Today, we will look at our concerns.

Questions (use all that time allows):

1. Can you give an example of something you wish had been done or said before your loved one died? If not, tell us about something that was resolved.
2. Do you handle unfinished business any differently now? If so, how?
3. Has attending church affected your grief journey? How?

4. Summary (5 minutes)

❖ Comment on what the group accomplished today.
❖ Announce the next session: Way of Suffering: *Golgotha*.
❖ Encourage *Participant Journal* work at home.
❖ Invite everyone to the Fellowship Finale.
❖ Pray "Prayer to the Giver of Hope" (group members listen and pray silently).

> O loving God,
> spirit of consolation and giver of hope,
> we thank you for the gift of your faithful people
> who join us today.
> We ask you to bless and keep them in your care.
> Let us also pray for the souls of our departed loved ones.
> (Pause so that group members may call these to mind.)
> May perpetual light shine upon them and bring eternal rest.
> We ask this through Christ our Lord.
> Amen.

5. Fellowship Finale (30 minutes)

SEASON

FOUR

Session FIVE
Way of Suffering

Theme: Golgotha

 Items Needed:

- pre-session music/player
- focal point: crucifix
- bibles
- *Participant Journal*
- *Maundy Thursday Gregorian Chant* (CD) by Monastic Choir of St. Peter's Abbey (optional)

1. Opening (10 minutes)

- ❖ Welcome the group and thank those who brought refreshments.
- ❖ Pray together the *"Seasons of Hope* Prayer."
- ❖ Seek feedback on the fourth *Participant Journal* home assignment: helping someone who is mourning.
- ❖ Ask if anyone brought a bereavement book or article to share and invite him or her to do so.

2. Activity (20 minutes)

 Script

This week we enter the Way of Suffering segment of *Seasons of Hope*. Let's turn to Mark 15:22–34 to encounter Jesus' crucifixion

on Golgotha, the place of the skull. (Have a teammate read the passage aloud while participants read along in their bibles.)

Christ's last moments on the cross portray extraordinary suffering of mind, body, and spirit. In his dying, Jesus speaks of feeling abandoned, something commonly experienced by those who mourn.

(Select music and exercise or the exercise alone.)

Music: (*Maundy Thursday* CD or music for meditation.)

Exercise: (Provide pencils.)

 Script

Let's open the *Participant Journal* to the Guidepost for session five.

1. Use your crucifix from home or gaze at the one on the prayer table to reflect on the Lord's final moments. Let him speak to your heart.
2. Jot down your thoughts in the *Participant Journal*.

I will signal when it's time to begin Faith Sharing.

3. Faith Sharing (45 minutes)

Questions (use all that time allows):

1. Did the circumstances of your loved one's final moments strengthen or shake your faith? Explain.
2. Has your loss brought to mind Jesus' question to the Father: "Why have you forsaken me?" Explain.
3. What is the most consoling thing Jesus could say to you?

SEASON
FOUR

4. Summary (5 minutes)

❖ Comment on what the group accomplished today.
❖ Announce the last session: Final Destination: *Be My Witnesses.*
❖ Ask participants to bring an item to the last session that symbolizes their love for the deceased.
❖ Encourage *Participant Journal* work at home.
❖ Invite everyone to the Fellowship Finale.
❖ Pray "Prayer to the Giver of Hope" (group members listen and pray silently).

> O loving God,
> spirit of consolation and giver of hope,
> we thank you for the gift of your faithful people
> who join us today.
> We ask you to bless and keep them in your care.
> Let us also pray for the souls of our departed loved ones.
> (Pause while group members call these to mind.)
> May perpetual light shine upon them and bring eternal rest.
> We ask this through Christ our Lord.
> Amen.

5. Fellowship Finale (30 minutes)

SEASON
FOUR

Session SIX
Final Destination

Theme: Be My Witnesses

 Items Needed:

- pre-session music/player
- prayer table with focal point
- bibles
- *Participant Journal*
- pencils
- camera
- item that symbolizes your love for the deceased

1. Opening (5 minutes)

- ❖ Welcome the group and thank those who brought refreshments.
- ❖ Pray together the *"Seasons of Hope Prayer."*
- ❖ Seek feedback on the fifth *Participant Journal* home assignment: praising the Lord.
- ❖ Ask if anyone brought a bereavement book or article to share and invite him or her to do so.

SEASON
FOUR

2. Activity (35 minutes)

(If the chairs are in rows, form a circle.)

 Script

Each week we honor our deceased loved ones with word and prayer. Today we go a step further.

1. I invite each of you to show something that reminds you of the love you shared with your departed loved one and tell why it is special to you.
2. Then place the item on the prayer table.

Who would like to go first? (Team shares last.)

Thank you for sharing. It's nice to know more about your loved ones. Now we'll focus on scripture.

Scripture (10 minutes)

Your stories are wonderful examples of the power of love. And love was the center of the Lord's teaching. Jesus shared a final teaching as he was about to ascend to heaven. Let's turn to Acts 1:6–11 to learn what he said.

(Have a teammate read the passage aloud while participants read along in their bibles.)

The grieving apostles, like many of us, had questions about the future. Jesus' reply affirmed what mourning teaches us: what lies ahead is a mystery to us. Nevertheless, we are to be his witnesses.

3. Faith Sharing (35 minutes)

Questions (use all that time allows):

1. By participating in *Seasons of Hope*, you have been the Lord's witnesses. How has faith sharing affected your grief?
2. Have others who mourn given you hope? In what way?
3. What hope have you shared with them?

4. Summary (10 minutes)

❖ Comment on group accomplishments this season and future *Seasons of Hope* offerings.

❖ Encourage *Participant Journal* work at home for the final week.

❖ Have participants do the Season Survey in the *Participant Journal* (or reproduced from the download at www.avemariapress.com) and collect them.

❖ Invite everyone to the Fellowship Finale.

❖ Pray "Prayer to the Giver of Hope." (group members listen and pray silently).

> O loving God,
> spirit of consolation and giver of hope,
> we thank you for the gift of your faithful people
> who join us today.
> We ask you to bless and keep them in your care.
> Let us also pray for the souls of our departed loved ones.
> (Pause so that group members may call these to mind.)
> May perpetual light shine upon them and bring eternal rest.
> We ask this through Christ our Lord.
> Amen.

Take a group photograph.

5. Fellowship Finale (30 minutes)

SEASON

FOUR

APPENDIX

A Christ-centered support group is for you if any of these are true:

- You are looking for friends in Christ to share your journey of sorrow

- You've been trying to figure out the meaning of your grief

- You want to get on with life but haven't been able to

- You find comfort in the teaching of Christ

- You are open to new ways of coping with your grief

- You don't want to feel alone anymore

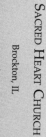

SEASONS OF HOPE

A Support
Group
for the
Bereaved

at

SACRED HEART CHURCH

Brockton, IL

APPENDIX

SEASONS OF HOPE
A Support Group for the Bereaved

Summer 2007

O ur Lord assured us that those who mourn are blessed, and that they shall be comforted. *Seasons of Hope* offers the bereaved an opportunity to come together to share in God's love. With the support of the faith community, we can give voice to our unique journeys of grief and find healing and spiritual growth. *Seasons of Hope* sessions help us explore mourning through scripture, prayer, reflection activities and faith sharing.

Seasons of Hope is centered on Jesus Christ and grounded in the healing wisdom, traditions, and practices of the Catholic Church.

Each year, many families face the loss of loved ones who are members of the parish. Our Catholic tradition provides funeral support and now *Seasons of Hope* can carry that caring spirit into the difficult period that follows when grief can overwhelm. It also serves those who mourn loved ones from outside our parish community. They too may feel isolated, empty, and broken-hearted.

For those searching for hope, a *Seasons of Hope* group is a nurturing link to the Church, the Almighty, and other people of faith who are also mourning.
Come and be comforted.

Seasons of Hope meets for six consecutive Sunday afternoons. Any parishioner who is mourning the loss of a loved one is encouraged to attend and invited to bring a guest. Please join us:

June 11, 18, & 25
and July 2, 9, & 16
at Sacred Heart Parish Center
Meeting Room A

* * *

- Sign in is from 3:30-3:55 pm
- The group meets from 4:00-6:00
- Please bring a bible.

* * *

For more information
or to register contact
Mary Davis at 555-XXXX

About the Seasons of Hope Team

(Brief sketches about the team or facilitators)

*Visit avemariapress.com to create your own brochure.

APPENDIX

1. Season One Sessions-at-a-Glance

Session	Theme	Opening	Activity	Faith Sharing	Summary & Fellowship
1. Point of Departure	*For Whom Are You Looking?*	20 minutes	20 minutes Jn 20:11–18 Get to know each other.	25 minutes Linking loss to the emotions of the saints	5 minutes 30 minutes
2. Path to Understanding	*Our Source of Consolation*	20 minutes	20 minutes Mt 11:28–30 Music: "My Yoke Is Easy" List what makes you weary.	35 minutes How God lightens burdens	5 minutes 30 minutes
3. Obstacles on the Journey	*Shattered Dreams*	10 minutes	15 minutes Jer 18:1–6 Music: "Abba Father"	40 minutes Honoring emotions and dreams	5 minutes 30 minutes
4. Path to Inner Healing	*Finding Joy*	10 minutes	20 minutes Jn 16:19–24 Write a letter to God to rekindle joy	40 minutes What helps in tough times	5 minutes 30 minutes
5. Way of Suffering	*The Way of The Cross*	5 minutes	20 minutes Lk 23:13–56 Music: *Chant* Stations of Cross	45 minutes Experiencing the Way of the Cross	5 minutes 30 minutes
6. Final Destination	*Untie Him*	5 minutes	35 minutes Jn 11:1–44 Share pictures	30 minutes Jesus and our ties to our departed	10 minutes (survey) 30 minutes

APPENDIX

2. Season Two Sessions-at-a-Glance

Session	Theme	Opening	Activity	Faith Sharing	Summary & Fellowship
1. Point of Departure	Remembering	20 minutes	20 minutes Lk 24:1–12 Walk down memory lane.	35 minutes Comparing reactions to scripture story	5 minutes 30 minutes
2. Path to Understanding	Seeking Consolation	15 minutes	20 minutes Jn 5:1–9 Music: "Song Over the Water" or "My Soul Thirsts" List what holds you back.	35 minutes What it takes to heal after loss	5 minutes 30 minutes
3. Obstacles on the Journey	Stumbling Blocks	10 minutes	20 minutes Is 57:14–15 Music: "Build Up" Select stones	40 minutes Moving these stones	5 minutes 30 minutes
4. Path to Inner Healing	Living Hope	10 minutes	15 minutes 1 Pt 1:3–9 Hand grief to Jesus.	45 minutes What sustains hope	5 minutes 30 minutes
5. Way of Suffering	The Cross	5 minutes	10 minutes Lk 9:22–24 Music: Chant Meditation on Rosary Crucifix	50 minutes Experiencing the Cross	5 minutes 30 minutes
6. Final Destination	Do Not Be Afraid	5 minutes	30 minutes Lk 8:40–42,49–56 Share memories.	35 minutes Inviting Jesus in	10 minutes (survey) 30 minutes

APPENDIX

3. Season Three Sessions-at-a-Glance

Session	Theme	Opening	Activity	Faith Sharing	Summary & Fellowship
1. Point of Departure	Believing	20 minutes	20 minutes Jn 20:24–29 Get to know each other.	35 minutes Exploring reactions to loss	5 minutes 30 minutes
2. Path to Understanding	Knock and the Door Shall Be Opened	20 minutes	20 minutes Mt 7:7–11 Draw picture. List what you need.	35 minutes How to receive	5 minutes 30 minutes
3. Obstacles on the Journey	Our Infirmities	15 minutes	15 minutes Lk 13:10–13 Music: "You Raise Me Up" or "We Will Rise" Imagine how it wil feel to have Jesus heal you.	40 minutes Being weighed down	5 minutes 30 minutes
4. Path to Inner Healing	Blinders to Faith	10 minutes	20 minutes Lk 18:35–43 Letter of petition to God	40 minutes How to find the way	5 minutes 30 minutes
5. Way of Suffering	His Wounds	10 minutes	15 minutes 1 Pt 2:20b–24 Music: "Maundy Thursday" Meditation: symbols	45 minutes What the calling means	5 minutes 30 minutes
6. Final Destination	Do Not Weep	5 minutes	30 minutes Lk 7:11–17 Share faith symbols.	40 minutes Drying the tears	10 minutes (survey) 30 minutes

4. Season Four Sessions-at-a-Glance

Session	Theme	Opening	Activity	Faith Sharing	Summary & Fellowship
1. Point of Departure	Last Encounter	20 minutes	20 minutes Jn 14:1–8 Get to know each other.	35 minutes Faith and coping.	5 minutes 30 minutes
2. Path to Understanding	The Garden of Gethsemane	20 minutes	15 minutes Mk 14:32–42 List your requests.	35 minutes Answers to our prayers	5 minutes 30 minutes
3. Obstacles on the Journey	Crown of Thorns	15 minutes	15 minutes Jn 19:1–3 Focus: rose Write what eased your pain.	44 minutes Roses among the thorns	5 minutes 30 minutes
4. Path to Inner Healing	Gift of Caring	15 minutes	20 minutes Jn 19:25–30 Letter of gratitude to God	40 minutes Unfinished business	5 minutes 30 minutes
5. Way of Suffering	Golgotha	10 minutes	20 minutes Mk 15:22–34 Music: "Maundy Thursday" Meditation: crucifix	45 minutes At the foot of the cross	5 minutes 30 minutes
6. Final Destination	Be My Witnesses	5 minutes	35 minutes Acts 1:6–11 Share symbol of love.	35 minutes Bearing witness	10 minutes (survey) 30 minutes

APPENDIX

5. Season One *Participant Journal-at-a-Glance*

Week	Theme	Scriptural Focus	Reflection	Journal Entry	Moving Forward
1. Point of Departure	Why Are You Weeping?	Jn 20:11–18 Meaning of loss	Use photo of happier time to focus on positive emotion	Thinks of tomb scene. Writes to Jesus about grief	Lights a candle for the deceased
2. Path to Understanding	Our Source of Consolation	Mt 11:28–30 Jesus and funeral as comfort	Remembers who/what lightened the burden at wake/funeral	Dialogues with God about current burden	Reaches out to someone
3. Obstacles on the Journey	Picking Up the Pieces	Jer 18:1–6 The Potter's hand in grief	Imagines a shattered pot and if it can be fixed	Describes brokenhearted feelings and seeks Jesus	Spends time before the Blessed Sacrament
4. Path to Inner Healing	Finding Joy	Jn 16:19–24 Weeping and mourning become joy	Thinks of joy before loss and whether God was included	Notes how deceased gave joy and impacted life	Rejoices about something this week
5. Way of Suffering	Bearing Your Cross	Lk 23:13–56 The cross of Christ	Gazes on a cross and ponders its meaning to the deceased and self	Shares own experiences of stumbling and falling with the cross	Thinks about each word and motion during the sign of the Cross
6. Final Destination	Letting God	Jn 11:1–44 Martha's handling of death; Jesus' teaching	Contemplates Jesus' tears	Lists complaints and searches for the glory of God in losing someone	Prays with incense

6. Season Two *Participant Journal-at-a-Glance*

Week	Theme	Scriptural Focus	Reflection	Journal Entry	Moving Forward
1. Point of Departure	*Disbelief*	Lk 24:1–12 The unexpected	Looks at memento of the deceased and focuses on positive emotion	Reviews how apostles reacted and writes to Jesus about own disbelief	Places memento with picture of deceased and offers a prayer
2. Path to Understanding	*Seeking Consolation*	Jn 5:1–9 Taking up our mat	Considers own grief journey	Dialogues with God about motivators to action	Prays for those who have helped
3. Obstacles on the Journey	*Stones for Building*	Is 57:14–15 Stones of life	Considers own grief journey	Writes about being crushed in spirit	Blesses and carries a stone this week
4. Path to Inner Healing	*Living Hope*	1 Pt 1:3–9 Our inheritance	Probes whether good can come from trials	Notes when hope entered own grief	Encourages someone
5. Way of Suffering	*Sorrow*	Lk 9:22–24 Fourth Sorrowful Mystery of the Rosary	Imagines Mary's sorrow as Jesus carried the cross	Shares own sorrow	Prays the Sorrowful Mysteries
6. Final Destination	*Just Have Faith*	Lk 8:40–42,49–56 Faith saves	Recalls bringing Jesus to the beloved	Thanks Jesus for his help	Kneels at the tabernacle to pray

APPENDIX

7. Season Three *Participant Journal-at-a-Glance*

Week	Theme	Scriptural Focus	Reflection	Journal Entry	Moving Forward
1. Point of Departure	*Doubting Thomas*	Jn 20:24–29 The encounter	Contemplates the sacred wounds	Writes thoughts about life after death	Visits the beloved's grave
2. Path to Understanding	*Open Doors*	Mt 7:7–11 Asking	Considers what God's will might be regarding grief	Dialogues with Jesus about trust	In prayer, beholds the door of the tabernacle
3. Obstacles on the Journey	*Crippled Spirit*	Lk 13:10–13 Bent with worry	Recognizes God's helping hand in mourning	Confides troubles	Seeks the sacrament of reconciliation
4. Path to Inner Healing	*Blind Faith*	Lk 18:35–43 Compassion	Asks if Jesus' pity has been sought	Tells Jesus how to help with grief	Helps someone who needs compassion
5. Way of Suffering	*Christ's Example*	1 Pt 2:20b–24 His footsteps	Explores how the deceased's life reflected God	Shares trying to follow the Lord	Asks for courage while receiving the Eucharist this week
6. Final Destination	*No Tears*	Lk 7:11–17 The power of Jesus	Recalls the funeral procession of the beloved	Acknowledges how Jesus touches grief	Arranges a memorial mass

APPENDIX

8. Season Four *Participant Journal-at-a-Glance*

Week	Theme	Scriptural Focus	Reflection	Journal Entry	Moving Forward
1. Point of Departure	*The Father's House*	Jn 14:1–8 Grasping the truth	Contemplates heaven	Writes about being left behind	Uses centering prayer
2. Path to Understanding	*Betrayal*	Mk 14:32–42 Keeping Watch	Reviews the positive support given to a loved one	Shares a difficult moment with the deceased	Genuflects mindfully
3. Obstacles on the Journey	*Suffering*	Jn 19:1–3 Injury	Considers the resurrected Christ	Considers how suffering through grief transforms	Receives communion from the cup
4. Path to Inner Healing	*Infinite Thirst*	Jn 19:25–30 Love	Focuses on the compassion of Christ	Explores responding to Jesus' thirst for love	Reaches out to someone in mourning
5. Way of Suffering	*Hurtful Words*	Mk 15:22–34 Jesus as victim	Ponders the power of words	Lifts up wounded feelings to the Lord	Praises the Lord
6. Final Destination	*Patience*	Acts 1:6–11 Waiting for the kingdom	Explores attitude toward patience	Tells Jesus what is hoped for now	Prays the Glorious Mysteries of the Rosary

Suggested Sound Recordings

Pre-session Instrumental Music:
Haugen, Marty. *Instruments of Peace.* GIA Publications
Simplicity: A Spiritual Instrumental Music Experience, volume 2-guitar. Pamplin Music Corporation
Simplicity Praise: An Instrumental Praise Experience, volume 3-harp and flute. Pamplin Music Corporation
Talbot, John Michael. *The Quiet Side.* The Sparrow Corporation

Additional Sources
www.catholicmusicnetwork.com (Catholic Music Network, 256-352-5045)
www.ocp.org (Oregon Catholic Press, Portland, OR / 800-548-8749)

Suggestions for Sessions

SEASON ONE

Session 2:
Talbot, John Michael. *Master Collection V.I The Quiet Side.* The Sparrow Corporation

Session 4:
Landry, Carey, and Carol Jean Kinghorn. *Abba, Father—Prayer Songs.* OCP Publications

Session 5:
The Benedictine Monks of Santo Domingo de Silos. *Chant.* Angel Records

SEASON TWO

Session 2:
Haugen, Marty. *Anthology II: The Best of Marty Haugen.* GIA Publications, Inc.
Schutte, Dan. *Lover of Us All.* NALR

Session 3:
Talbot, John Michael. *The Regathering.* The Sparrow Corporation

APPENDIX

Session 5:
The Benedictine Monks of Santo Domingo de Silos. *Chant*. Angel Records

SEASON THREE

Session 3:
Groban, Josh. *Closer*. Reprise Records
Talbot, John Michael, and Terry Talbot. *No Longer Strangers*. The Sparrow Corporation

Session 5:
Monastic Choir of St. Peter's Abbey, Solesmes. *Maundy Thursday: Gregorian Chant*. Creative Joys, Inc.

SEASON FOUR

Session 5:
Monastic Choir of St. Peter's Abbey, Solesmes. *Maundy Thursday: Gregorian Chant*. Creative Joys, Inc.

Helpful Resources for the Team

BOOKS

Chilson, Richard. *Prayer: Exploring a Great Spiritual Practice*. Notre Dame, IN: Ave Maria, 2006.
Ebeling, Carol Fredericks. *What to Say: 52 Positive Ways to Show Christian Sympathy to Those Who Grieve*. St. Louis: Concordia, 2002.
Fitzgerald, Helen. *The Mourning Handbook: The Most Comprehensive Resource Offering Practical and Compassionate Advice on Coping With All Aspects of Death and Dying*. New York: Fireside, 1995.
Icenogle, Gareth Weldon. *Biblical Foundations for Small Group Ministry: An Integrative Approach*. Downers Grove, IL: InterVarsity, 1994.
Irish, Donald P., and Kathleen F. Lundquist. *Ethnic Variations in Dying, Death, and Grief: Diversity in Universality*. London: Routledge, 1993.
Jones, Laurie Beth. *Jesus, CEO: Using Ancient Wisdom for Visionary Leadership*. New York: Hyperion, 1995.
McBride, Neal F. *How to Lead Small Groups*. Colorado Springs, CO: Navpress, 1990.
National Catholic Ministry to the Bereaved Training Manual, New Edition. St. Louis: National Catholic Ministry to the Bereaved, 2007.
Nelson, Jan, and David Aaker. *The Bereavement Ministry Program: A Comprehensive Guide for Churches*. Notre Dame: Ave Maria, 1998.
Parkes, Colin, Pittu Laungani, and Bill Young, editors. *Death and Bereavement Across Cultures*. London: Routledge, 1997.

APPENDIX

Sullivan, James. *The Good Listener*. Notre Dame, IN: Ave Maria, 2000.

Wheeler, Marion, editor. *His Face: Images of Christ in Art*. New York: Chameleon Books, 1988.

Williams, Donna Reilly and JoAnn Sturzi. *Grief Ministry: Helping Others Mourn*. San Jose, CA: Resource, 1992–2000.

Worden, J. William. *Grief Counseling and Grief Therapy: A Handbook for the Mental Health Practitioner*. New York: Springer, 2002.

ORGANIZATIONS

AARP
www.aarp.org/families/grief_loss/
601 E St., Washington, DC 20049
888-687-2277

Association for Death Education and Counseling
www.adec.org
324 N. Main St., W.
Hartford, CT 06117
860-586-7503

International Parish Nurse Resource Center
www.parishnurses.org
314-918-2557

National Catholic Ministry to the Bereaved
www.griefwork.org
PO Box 16353
St. Louis, MO 63125
314-638-2638

APPENDIX

M. Donna MacLeod, RN, MSN, a certified bereavement specialist and hospice professional, began *Seasons of Hope* support groups in 1990. Inspired by the loss of her youngest daughter, Erynne, and the compassionate response of her parish in New England, MacLeod felt called to minister to those who mourn.

A seasoned lecturer and facilitator, MacLeod has organized parish bereavement ministries across the country. She now volunteers for the Diocese of Orlando. A member of the local chapter of the Association for Death Education and Counseling, she also serves on the Board of Trustees for the National Catholic Ministry to the Bereaved.

She was motivated to write *Seasons of Hope Guidebook* by participants in the Oregon Seasons of Hope program who mentioned how beneficial they felt her materials could be to friends and family around the country.

MacLeod enjoys motherhood, grandparenthood, and residing in Florida and on Cape Cod with husband, Bryan. She can be reached through seasonsofhope@cfl.rr.com.